Messenger for the Guardians

A Psychic's Journey into Angelic Communication

by
Martin E. Crespo

Bloomington, IN   Milton Keynes, UK

AuthorHouse™
1663 Liberty Drive, Suite 200
Bloomington, IN 47403
www.authorhouse.com
Phone: 1-800-839-8640

AuthorHouse™ UK Ltd.
500 Avebury Boulevard
Central Milton Keynes, MK9 2BE
www.authorhouse.co.uk
Phone: 08001974150

© *2008 Martin E. Crespo. All rights reserved.*

No part of this book may be reproduced, stored in a retrieval system, or transmitted by any means without the written permission of the author.

First published by AuthorHouse 11/13/2008

ISBN: 978-1-4389-3210-1 (hc)
ISBN: 978-1-4259-3800-0 (sc)

Library of Congress Control Number: 2006904491

Printed in the United States of America
Bloomington, Indiana

This book is printed on acid-free paper.

This book is dedicated to my wife and son who inspire me to reach for the stars on a daily basis. To all those individuals who believed in me and gave me the courage to believe in my work. It is also to acknowledge our Guardian angels, those beautiful beings of light and love, who constantly surround us with unconditional love.

Table of Contents

Introduction ix

Chapter 1   Awakening to Spirituality 1

Chapter 2   Guardian Angels 7

Chapter 3   First Message: Fear 19

Chapter 4   Second Message: Acceptance 33

Chapter 5   Third Message: Health 43

Chapter 6   Fourth Message: Focus 57

Chapter 7   Fifth Message: Letting Go 67

Chapter 8   Sixth Message: Expressing 77

Chapter 9   Seventh Message: Mergence 85

Chapter 10   Eighth Message: Group Consciousness 99

Chapter 11   Ninth Message: Children 111

Chapter 12   Tenth Message: Love 123

Chapter 13   Time To React 139

Introduction

As mankind's overall evolution continues, so does his desire to understand himself more, especially spiritually. We have reached a point where we wish to see and understand the total picture and not just bits and pieces. Scientists, physicists, and engineers pry deeper into the makeup of our physical planet while others continue searching for unlimited potentials of life in our oceans and in our galaxy. Many of us have decided to stop reaching out to the stars, and have started going within ourselves in order to gain contact with our souls. We are living in a most intriguing era of Spiritual discovery. We are finally realizing the importance of going within ourselves in order to discover the nature of our spiritual being. For centuries we have marched forward into our physical environment to seek knowledge in areas of technology, space, medicine, and global affairs. Now we are being instructed by a higher knowing to stop going out into the universe and start going within ourselves. With the Age of Aquarius upon us, we open to a new heightened sense of life, a life that is not physical, but rather spiritual. As we continue to destroy our resources, wage wars over difference of opinions, climb the social and monetary ladder, many of us have ventured in search of our soul's purpose and recognition.

Over the last twenty years humanity has been engulfed with religious and spiritual wake up calls. Sightings of the blessed Virgin Mary have been reported throughout all areas of the world, regardless of religious origins. Fascination with Angels, God, and the Devil in movie themes, television shows, books, lectures, have been even more extremely popular over the last ten years. We have realized that we can no longer keep evolving unless we seek outside guidance. Now, more than ever, this outside guidance is reaching out to us unlike any other time in the history of our planet. We are finally accepting our roles as extensions of our God Source as well as understanding the importance of love and the need for it to survive. Guided by wonderful beings of unconditional love and light, we are looking forward to establishing communication and contact with our angels, in order to align ourselves with our missions as individuals, and as a group consciousness.

I have been involved in psychic and spiritual encounters since the age of seven and a half, and now some forty years later, I have realized that all my experiences were not necessarily for my own growth, but rather to be shared among others for our independent and planetary growth. Forced to question my mental stability at a young age, due to all the strange experiences I was encountering, I always knew I was being watched or guided throughout the process. In my struggles to have an understanding of my fears and doubts, I separated myself from the world because I felt I did not belong. Now, after spending many years teaching others about Spirituality and metaphysical topics, I have come to realize I was not really different from others. I have finally understood that I was simply more open to certain encounters because it would hold a purpose in my future.

Years of seeing and communicating with angels, in particular, Guardian angels, have led me to write this book. I write these words to show others that we are never alone, we are loved unconditionally in a way we can never understand, and every one of us serve a purpose of utmost importance throughout our lives. As years passed, and I was able to pass down information to thousands of individuals from their Guardian angels, I accepted my role as a messenger. I share in this book insights, experiences, and words of love, in order to awaken the ability for all of us to release fear and trust ourselves more. More importantly, I write this book to help us understand how valuable we all are to the future of this planet, the future of the Spiritual plane, and the future of all dimensions leading to our God Source.

Chapter 1

Awakening to Spirituality

The new millennium came and went a few years ago without any of the anticipated technological disasters or world ending events. In actuality, something dramatic did take place, but it didn't arrive at the stroke of midnight as we shifted into the year 2000. It actually crept in a few years earlier, when we first began thinking of the new millennium, and what it would bring into our world. Instead of chaos and world ending catastrophes, we were introduced to an era of questioning and disillusionment. Believe it or not, there were many individuals on this planet, who were hoping that the entry of the year 2000 would have taken their lives. This would have given them a reason to excuse themselves from responsibilities and hardships which they could not endure anymore. Others faced this shift as an opportunity to witness a spiritual awakening and were left disappointed. For them, this anticipated awakening of a spiritual slumber which never appeared, left them wondering what went wrong.

Not having our responsibilities taken away from us by God or technological disasters, forced us to analyze ourselves. We realized that God and technology were not going to make things any easier than they were before the year 2000. We also realized that in order to continue surviving we had to seek new guidelines. This realization was actually one of the best gifts that we could have possibly received. We, as human beings, were forced to seek alternative ways to take control of our lives. Realizing that a special care package was not going to be left on our doorsteps, we had to take the initiative to stop depending on someone or something else from the outside world, and look within for answers. We were finally forced to grow up.

As a psychic, I was also caught in this time frame of questioning and wondering, and felt I should have been given some insights. I felt cheated that I had not been shown or given advance notice of new things to come. As most psychics will tell you, we have yet to discover that magical fountain of all-knowing information. Fielding questions from my clients, friends, family members, and people who attended my lectures, I realized something indeed had changed. Humanity had changed! Looking at me, as a man who had access to future events, people wanted a direct answer. They did not want just a general run of the mill reply, but a detailed, prove it to me, I better be satisfied, type of response! I could sense an urgency in their tone but could not really grasp why it was also coated with anger. A few months later, as we came close to entering the year 2001 I finally realized something had shifted. As the year unfolded, my clients continued to demand more and more from my sessions, forcing me to demand more of myself. I knew that my work with Guardian angels had taken a new profound meaning.

I am not referring to the Guardian angels which walk around the city of New York for years assisting with the crime epidemic. I am referring literally to Angels, those floating, loving beings of light, who watch over all of us throughout our lives. This was the gift that destiny placed upon me, the ability to see and communicate with individual's Guardian angels since I was a child. The realization that came to me at the end of the year 2001 was that I was not here to provide answers to individual people from their Angels, but rather in the process of doing just that, I was here to provide messages to humanity! Humanity was ready to change and wanted step by step instructions to create this change. The more I continued to do one on one sessions, normally called readings, the more I realized that many of the answers the Guardian Angels were giving to these people could actually apply to all of us, including myself!

My life was also going through many transitions and like many of my clients, I also was dealing with issues of financial difficulties, work changes, and personal love issues. I began applying some of the strategies that the Angels were telling my clients to do to my own existence. Suddenly, I was hit with a higher level of clarity and understanding than I had ever experienced in my forty two years. I had to make some very important decisions, and needed to take charge, and rearrange my life. Things started to fall into place so much easier, I felt a huge weight lift from my shoulders, and I could no longer blame negative issues in my life on an outside Source. I realized, God, my family, or life in general, had nothing to do with me being in the state of existence which I was. Decisions, fears, acceptance issues, health problems, communication blockages, and many other areas of my life which I controlled and initiated, had played a key role in creating the person I had become.

Suddenly, I became more and more interested in what these Guardian Angels were telling my clients for I realized I was being given the privilege of listening to some very valuable and life changing information. I also looked at the confirmations that my clients were giving me in relation to the information being told to them. Over and over these individuals were walking away from my office crying tears of relief derived from their own level of understanding and clarity. This was the same clarity I also was experiencing as I continued following the guidelines set by our Angelic helpers.

The challenge facing me now was my ability to retain as much of the information provided by the angels, and put it into some kind of constructive form. You see, after doing readings for so many years, I placed a request from my own angel, which now made it difficult to capture and hold all the information I provided during a reading. When I first started doing readings, I would remember word for word everything that was discussed in each session. I consider myself to be a very sensitive person, and I would go home worried about the teenager suffering from cancer, or the poor gentleman who lost his child in a car accident, not to mention the lady who was fifty six years old and claims to have never felt or experienced love in her whole life. After years of taking home other people's personal issues and worries, I asked my angel if they could possibly delete much of the information that I was providing and hearing with my clients. I didn't want to take such a huge emotional load home. Through time, my need to retain all the information discussed in my readings, became less and less.

I receive my information from the Guardian Angel, who usually stands behind or to the side of my client, in a telepathic form. I do not get word by word details, instead, I get the entire concept in one big paragraph in a matter of two or three seconds. This information is enhanced with visual images I receive, as well as, emotional feelings which run through my body. Now suddenly, I wanted to retain all that was being shared in my readings, in order to analyze and understand how these messages played out in all of our lives. I asked permission from some of the clients if I could make a copy of the cassette normally provided to them with the information of the reading and I started replaying them later on at my house. I began building a series of messages which I felt were important for all of humanity. I decided to take, what I considered to be the top ten messages, and create a simple and instructive book which the reader could use as a manual to discover ways of taking charge of their life once again. It will also assist them in changing bad habits which we all have when it comes to dealing with changes in our existence. As human beings, we have a tendency to look at changes as negative experiences connected to hidden trap doors.

I hope to take you on a journey where you, while reading these words, will feel as though you are right in my office along with your Guardian Angel in what can be a wonderful session into self discovery. Each message flows into the next one and your ability to apply them to your own existence is what will make this journey a triumphant one.

We are living in a time where our faith is being tested in many ways. The foundation of organized religion seems to be shaky and a desire for individual Spiritual growth has emerged. Remember that Spirituality is an individual's hunger to discover their God in association to themselves, while religion is a group experience sometimes controlled by one or too few. We are walking into a new era of information and resources. We are entering a world of soul searching and compassion unlike anything ever before and we need to decide if we wish to participate in this journey. Allow your own Guardian Angel to lead you, for we all have one, and allow them to highlight in your heart the message or messages which will assist you the most.

There are many levels of angels which have existed throughout time. This book focuses on the messages of our Guardian angels, our army of loving soldiers, who are dedicated to our individual growth. Understand that every one of these messages has enough information that each one can be a separate book. I am simply touching on the highlights of each message. There are other messages from the angels which I have decided not to include in this book because they are geared towards future upcoming events which the angels felt should be placed on hold until a later date. Our angels simply want to let us know how much we are loved and how capable we are of existing in harmony upon this complicated world we have created. The next chapter is dedicated to answering many of the questions we all have in trying to understand Guardian angels. So strap yourself in, you might hit a few bumpy roads as you take this journey, but realize your copilot is your Guardian angel sitting right by your side. With this copilot, you are bound to land smoothly, but things might just not look the same anymore by the time you finish the ride!

Chapter 2

Guardian Angels

In this chapter I hope to provide an insight into the framework of our Guardian angels and answer questions so often presented to me. To begin with, not only special chosen individuals have a Guardian angel, all humans have their own spiritual protector. Regardless of race, color, religious background, or personal belief you might have, your Guardian angel is by your side throughout your entire lifetime. This being of love will never change or abandon you, for it is assigned to your existence, and will unconditionally continue to pour love and wisdom into your heart, mind, and soul with relentless passion. There are other beings in the spiritual realm who also, at times, enter your life to lend a helping hand or provide insights. I like to refer to them as Spirit guides and teachers. They are composed of family members and friends who have passed on, other levels of angels who temporarily touch our lives, and spiritual teachers who coexist in various spiritual planes.

All of the information I will provide to you comes from years of communicating with individuals' Guardian angels in personal consultations or readings, classes, workshops I have done, physical healing work on myself and others, and at times unexpected experiences, which have changed my life. I have gathered the most common questions asked from people who want clarity or a better understanding of their Guardian angels, those who simply wish to work with their own angel, and of course those who are skeptic to their existence in general. Remember, many of these answers come directly from the Guardian angels themselves!

When does my Guardian angel decide to connect with my existence?

In order to answer this question, I first need to explain what happens to us when we die. We all will play the same role when our time comes. All of us will eventually leave this physical body and move into spirit form upon our death. Regardless of the way you died, what you did or didn't do while you were alive, does not remove you from this process. We, upon accepting our deaths, will go through an evaluation of our existence based on a quick review of all the experiences we had while in human form. The beauty of this is that our Creator or God, whom I will refer to from this point forward as the Source, allows us to judge our own life. When we die, we enter a level of spiritual existence in which we cannot hide anything from ourselves, therefore we will acknowledge all our mistakes, errors, bad decisions, as well as the good we have performed.

Next, we proceed to enter the spiritual realm, where this is most commonly experienced as a journey through a tunnel of pure light. Upon passing through the other side of this tunnel we are greeted by loved ones which have crossed over before us, as well as other beautiful beings of light and love. The final phase of this death process is where we accumulate what we have learned from our most recent physical life, and decide what areas we failed to accomplish important missions, or what situations in our life were left unfulfilled. We take the time to design a new game plan, a new physical life purpose in a new body, which will give our soul a sense of completion. We work out all the details, including the people we wish to be connected with at birth, the location we wish to enter in this planet, and all the experiences which we feel will be necessary to be met in order for our soul to revolutionize even further. The only kink in this great plan is that once we are born, all this information is pushed back into our subconscious mind and we have no recollection.

This is where your Guardian angel comes to play a role in your life. Right before you were born, based on what you wish to accomplish or experience, your Guardian angel joins with you in your entry to human form. They are here to assist you in accomplishing what you have chosen to do. They have access to your life mission and goals which you no longer have in your conscious mind. Realize time, as we experience and know it, has no existence in the spiritual realm. For your angel to be by your side forty, fifty, or eighty years is no trouble at all. This explanation of the death process is very real for me, for once, while battling a serious health issue, I had a near death experience. I had a chance to go through these steps of death myself. It was a very positive feeling, and like others who have gone through this, it is very difficult to leave this dimension of love and come back to physical form. I was told my mission had not really been touched, and I needed to return to the physical world.

Is my Guardian angel with me every single second of my life?

Your Guardian angel is connected with your soul every second of your life. What this means is that they do not necessarily have to be two feet away from you, twenty-four hours a day, in order to accomplish their work with you. They exist in a spiritual plane or dimension where they can communicate and interact with other angels, while at the same time keep their eyes on your development. They are also working on their own development at a much higher level. I don't want you to think that you are taking a long hot shower and your angel is sitting on the floor by the tub saying, "Ok, Ok, let's go, we have things to do!" They are at your side, while you are performing your daily chores, and at times they are busy handling other duties. Always remember, the moment you are engulfed in fear, feel lost or hurt, angry, or any other difficult experience, they are right next to you helping you overcome whatever obstacle has risen in your path.

Martin E. Crespo

Is my Guardian angel related to me? Could it be a grandparent or other older family member?

Ninety-nine percent of the time there is no connection between you and your Guardian angel. On a rare occasion there may exist a connection from a past life incident. As I mentioned before, they are with you right before you are even physically born, so if your grandfather passed away when you were two, he could not be your Guardian angel. He could be one of many Spirit guides who could enter in your life at different points. Your Guardian angels, like us, evolve and gain insights in certain areas more than others. Based on what you chose as your experiences in this life, your angel chooses you according to their area of expertise.

Where exactly do these angels come from, and are their different types of Guardian angels?

Some of our Guardian angels earn this responsibility or position, and others have chosen this responsibility from the beginning of time. This is where I need you to keep an open mind. When life was created billions and billions of years ago, the Source broke away from all-knowing energy in order to gain self experience. In other words, God or the Source had all knowledge, but lacked the experience of obtaining it. For example, let us say you wake up tomorrow and can play the piano like a professional, though you have never even sat in front of one in your life. Yes, it is a great feat, but you will lack the individual learning mechanism that led to this ability. Many levels or dimensions were created by the Source, in order to gain this learning mechanism or experience, from highly evolved spiritual planes down to the physical human level we exist in.

As these levels or dimensions were created, some chose to stay at a high evolved plateau, while others chose to venture even further down in this evolutionary plan. Various angelic realms or levels were created. At one of these levels, certain branches of angels were created, so that their main responsibility would be to give assistance to humans throughout their entire life. These are our present Guardian angels. Others were created to interact with humans at different intervals instead of dedicating all their energy to one individual. These angels have existed throughout time doing just that, assisting humans in their lives in one form or another. Those who chose to work solely with one person are the ones I refer to as Guardian angels.

Now, we also have Guardian angels who have escalated or graduated to this position. All of us as human beings have the right to reach a point in our lives, where upon death and review of our existence, we realize we have no need to come back for another round of human experience. The theory of regressions and past lives has been proven over and over, and as we gather more and more insights of love and humanity through various lives, we eventually will decide not to return. Once this decision is made, we stay in the spiritual realm, and with time and obviously more knowledge, we can at one point decide to be someone's Guardian angel. I have had the pleasure of communicating with these types of Guardian angels who lived countless lives and eventually decided not to come back and assist someone else in their physical journey. This does not make them any less powerful or knowing than those who have never incarnated in a human body. In fact, these angels can relate a bit more to the many hardships we have as human beings, for they have also endured them. One thing I have noticed, which I find to be humorous, is the existence of what I call "Rookie Guardian Angels", or those who are working with a human for the first time as their Guardian. The difference between these angels and others is not their knowledge but their hesitance in giving me information. It is almost as though they want to make sure that the information they are providing is so perfect that delays and pauses are more evident in their conversations. I also notice that the bright light of energy around these Rookies is a bit dimmer than the experienced Guardian angels. One thing that is both common and consistent in all levels of guardian angels, is their unconditional love.

How much does my Guardian angel know about me and can they change my destiny?

These two questions are very intriguing. Your angel knows more about you than you actually know about yourself. What this means is that they know all your weaknesses, fears, ambitions, loves, strengths, down to the very core of your soul. They do not judge you at all rather, they use this knowledge to assist you in your life mission. They also know you have one element of human existence which they will never interfere with, and that is your free will. They will never force you to do something you do not wish to do, and they will never change things in your path or in your destiny which are part of your lessons even if they are coated with fear, health issues, despair, hardships, or challenges. The reason they do not interfere with your destiny is because these experiences are the ones you set for the growth of your soul.

Your Guardian angel simply places people, situations, experiences, opportunities, and crossroads ahead of you to push you into the direction of knowledge you requested in this life. Your free will allows you to connect or ignore what they have placed in front of you. Free will and decisions you make in life will assist you in receiving their messages, and connect with your mission, or force you to lose out on a valuable life lesson. Your angel will keep trying again and again, even if it takes your whole lifetime to finally gain that particular experience or lesson. What your angel will also attempt to do is, warn you of an impending danger, or try to give you insights into future changes coming your way. This leads into the next question.

Does my Guardian angel attempt to communicate with me?

A quick answer to this question would be, YES! Every single day of your life your angel is trying to reach out to you. This is why it is so emotional for them during my consultation. Many times your Guardian angel is more excited and emotional to meet you and share words with you, than you are. Remember, they are with you throughout your life, enjoying all you accomplish and suffering all your hardships by your side. Through me, they are finally able to speak to you one on one, with no interferences. The love they pour out during these sessions is sometimes so powerful, I find myself with tears rolling down my face. During the time we are together in a session, I am connected to your angels' emotions, and I feel what your angel feels.

Outside of my ability to bring contact with you and your angel, there are other ways in which you can communicate with your angel. Dreams are very powerful tools they use to reach out to us. They provide insights, warnings, ideas, or simple greetings in our dreams. When you get a gut feeling, a sense of knowing something is about to happen, a hunch, or a premonition, that is usually your Guardian angel speaking with you. Sometimes we hear an inner voice whispering to us, but unfortunately, most of the time we ignore it. Many times that voice is your angel. Two ways to assist you in opening communication with your angel is meditation and automatic writing. Meditation allows you to filter and remove garbage thoughts that run randomly through your mind. It separates them from your consciousness, and in turn, allows you to tap into words of wisdom from your angels. Meditation allows you to enter into your subconscious, where you have stored information about your life mission and goals for this life. Besides allowing you to release stress, meditation can open a bridge between you and your angel for ongoing communications.

Automatic writing is a technique in which you allow your physical body and mind to join forces, and use written words as a form of communication with your angel. The easiest way, taught to me from a business partner, is to simply draw a line down the middle of a blank page. On the left side write any question you might have, and as soon as a random thought comes in a form of an answer jot it down on the right side of the line. Even if it feels you are just making it up, continue going from one question to the next, and do not read your answers until you have finished with all your questions. With practice, what you will notice, is that some of the words or phrases you have written on the right side are not normal words and phrases which you use in your everyday vocabulary. Do not expect your hand to be controlled by your angel and be forced to write. You must allow yourself to trust what comes down to your mind and simply write it.

Developing the psychic abilities we all have, will of course, further develop your ability to communicate with your Guardian angel. Trusting your intuition, building a regimen of meditations into your hectic schedule, keeping a dream journal, and looking for so-called coincidences in your life will help you discover just how much influence your angel has throughout your day. The sound of bells, having angelic figurines throughout the house, and simply wanting to listen to them will further enhance their ability to break the barriers that exist between our dimension and theirs.

Is there a difference between sex, race, or color between one Guardian Angel and another?

In my countless experiences and encounters with Guardian angels I have seen both male and female, all colors, sizes, races, and varying ages. Please take into consideration that their physical nature is of no importance to them, for in reality they are energy beings. They provide an image for us to relate to. In actuality, they are androgynous, having a balance between both male and female energy within their spiritual makeup. Some of the angels who have had physical incarnations will choose to appear to me in the image of one of the lives in which they felt the strongest, or accomplished the most. They choose the age where they felt they were at their highest peak in that particular life.

Some angels will choose the image of the last physical incarnation they had while on our planet. For example, if their last physical life was that of a man who lived in the 1400's, and who had died at the age of seventy, he might use the image of that life when he felt the strongest, possibly at the age of thirty. Those who have never existed in human form will take on an image, which they feel will be more accepting of the person they are watching over. What I have noticed though is that the image of a female Guardian angel will appear sixty to seventy percent of the time. I feel this is due to the fact that the male species has not yet developed the area of sensitivity and communication, which the female has. Nothing against men, but we still have not mastered the art of communication.

The same idea, using images which will appeal to the person, also applies to the names they wish to be called. Many times when I relate the name of the Guardian angel to the person I am consulting, they tell me it is their favorite name, it is the name they always wanted to use if they had a child, or it is the name of a friend or relative they really love and admire. In their dimension, these angels do not have names, they relate to each other in a telepathic sense through the vibration of love. We, as humans, depend on names to differentiate one individual from another. This has also led to separating the essence of one human being from another. In the angelic realm you begin to develop a sense of group consciousness where they exist in oneness.

One day, in our physical realm, we will also entertain this consciousness of working together as one.

Do all our Guardian angels have the same understanding and resource of information?

Again, in one word, Yes! They all have access to our past lives, emotions, fears, upcoming events, and all levels of experiences we have attained throughout our existence. When I am doing a reading with a person's Guardian angel, I do not get a voice, word by word information, or a sentence for that matter. What I receive during my sessions is a vibration of energy, which connects with my heart and soul, and suddenly I am engulfed in a whole paragraph of information, feelings, and visual images. All of this is provided to me in one vibration which takes two to three seconds. These vibrations are thrown at me one after the other thus, forcing me to speak about ninety miles an hour. I have to gather this telepathic thought, convert it into words which will be understood by my client, and try not to lose any data in between one vibration and the next. This is where my ability to interpret the data is so important, if I am thrown off a bit by the speed of the information, the timing of certain events or the accuracy of information may be altered a bit. Even with all this, from the countless feedback I have received from individuals after my sessions, they are amazed at the overall accuracy of information they receive. I also love to get feedback from upcoming events which are later confirmed to me by my clients.

If destiny does exist, why do we need these Guardian angels, shouldn't we simply follow the Universal plan set for each of us?

Destiny must be looked upon as the ultimate goal. How we go about reaching that goal has countless possibilities. Assisting us in reaching that goal with the least amount of hardship, and the highest level of experience is what our Guardian angels attempt to do for us. Being a man, I will use an example in the sports world to illustrate what this means. You have a football team whose ultimate goal is, win as many games as possible, reach the playoffs, and win a championship. What do we use to incorporate this plan and make it successful? We hire coaches, with various levels of expertise. Some of these coaches work with physical training, others with diet, while others are in charge of creating and teaching different tactics and plays to be used during the games. Well, consider your Guardian angel as your life coach!

Are these Guardian angels different in personality?

Yes, I have seen all levels of personalities, from those with straight one and two word answers, practical jokers wishing to share a sense of humor during difficult times, up to very emotional caring ones who take the time and gentleness to explain difficult situations coming. They know it is not easy surviving in this planet, and therefore, they incorporate different ways to get their messages across. Some of these angels become so emotionally involved, that at times, I ask them to cut back on the emotional energy going through my energetic body, and focus more on the information they have to provide. Not that this is bad on their part, but it can be draining on my mind and body.

Finally, do our Guardian angels have wings?

Sorry to disappoint you, but no, they do not come down fluttering their wings inside of my office. I have had only a handful of experiences in which I have seen wings on an angel but rarely on a Guardian angel. They look like you and me, except for an enormous brilliant glow of light which emits from their body. They can be easily disguised to walk among us if they so choose. On an average, many of them appear as individuals in their late twenties to early thirties. I have also seen Guardian angels in their late teens, as well as late sixties!

The next portion of this book, which I feel holds the highest value of information, consists of ten messages which have been shared to many individuals throughout all my readings with Guardian angels. I have gathered insights, wisdom, and beautiful expressions of love shared in experiences, stories, meditations, and exercises. I hope that as you read and follow along in this angelic journey, your heart, soul, and mind will expand as you discover more about yourself. I hope to offer you tools to assist you in releasing obstacles in your surroundings, but more importantly, to let you know you are never alone in this path we call life. Your Guardian angel has arranged for this book to fall into your hands and as far as I am concerned, nothing happens by chance. Your Guardian angel can be your closest friend, your work partner, your coach, your source of inspiration and self awareness, as long as you allow them. As you read and work through some of these messages, try to see yourself as the unlimited spiritual being you are. The messages are not placed in any specific order of importance for each one of them have their own unique value in our existence.

Chapter 3

First Message: Fear

There is one common factor which resonates with just about every client who decides to call me, and set up an appointment to speak with their Guardian angel. They all carry a high level of fear in their lives. Not a fear of meeting their angel, but an internal fear, connected with life in general. In actuality, we all have fear issues in our lives, we just adapt or try to disguise them. So, please feel normal if you wake up in the middle of the night wondering how the next stack of bills will be paid, how you will survive another day with the pain in your lower back, or if the person sleeping next to you will continue loving you ten years from now. There is even the possibility that upon meeting your angel, you will have the fear of thinking they are going to reprimand or scold you for some actions you have done in the past. Relax, they never do that, they are here to guide us, not punish us. Throughout the thousands of readings I have done so far, fear usually plays a very important role, unfortunately a destructive one.

Your angel will explain to you that fear was never meant to be part of the overall human package. Fear is the most non-productive source of energy we can possibly connect with. Mankind has allowed it to blossom to the point that it controls much of what we do and say in our lives. Fear was not provided to us when we entered this world. Instead, fear was taught to us, by society, our parents, and our inability to accept changes. The main reason fear is so destructive is that it goes against one of the most powerful forces available to us. That powerful force, known as love, is pushed away from you when you give in to your fears. The negativity that fear has over all of us, can eventually, be strong enough to last from one lifetime to another!

Throughout the beginning of time man has challenged himself to evolve, and in that process of attempting to be more civilized and technologically advanced, he has slowed down at various intervals because of fear. Fear creates doubt, which in turn creates lack of faith, which eventually turns into stagnant energy. For millions of years this fear has forced mankind to hide in the shadows and wonder who is in control and who is running the show. Due to physical limitations against nature, huge animals which could destroy us, and mental mistakes we did over and over, we created a sense of caution and worry going back to the caveman. This caution and worry escalated until we eventually turned it into fear. Once the fear was experienced several times, it became necessary for us to prepare others or our children, in anticipation.

Mankind began to teach fear to their young ones, at an early stage of their development, thinking they were preparing them to avoid danger. Little did they know that they were actually programming the young ones to anticipate fear even when there was no call for it. We did not understand that if fear was not part of our normal birth experience, by introducing it, we were simply creating a level of limitation in our existence. For example, a young child will not exhibit a level of fear when it gets hurt. It cries from the pain and discomfort it received at the point of the incident. The parents instruct the child on the possibility of what could happen at a higher level of pain if they do this again. In other words we hear, "Stay away from that cabinet, because next time, instead of just cutting your knee, the whole thing can come down on you and you will end up in the hospital with a broken leg." As you can see, parents are psychics, and they know how much worse things can get ahead of time! You and I entered this world with a desire to experience. This desire is the primary reason we even enter into a new life.

Experience will eventually bring about confusion and changes, and these are actually good things. If you are confused about something it means you are balancing ideas, thoughts, and emotions, this is called being human. If you are presented with changes this means opportunities and new experiences are being provided for you, and you need to discover them.

Your Guardian angel will explain to you that there are two levels of fear which we primarily deal with. One, is the fear of an existing action or process, and two, a predetermined fear implanted within us. The one we will be focusing on in this chapter is the second one. This is the one which is paralyzing mankind today in all levels of life. Men and women in general, due to high demands placed upon them by society, feel inadequate at various points of their lives. These inadequate feelings can be related to areas of physical attraction, financial income level, degree of power, social class status, and even religious and spiritual knowledge. We have a tendency to judge ourselves according to what we see around us, instead of what we carry inside.

We live in a time where we are bombarded by visual images. Television viewing, especially between children and teenagers, is higher now than ever before. The issues distributed on our television screens are violence, power, perfect specimens of human anatomy, and shows which feed off fear concepts. Because of expectations thrown at us, a warped sense of what holds truth and value in our society, and our self created fears, many of us see our lives as failures. Once we develop a false sense that others are better, we begin to focus more on our flaws, and worst of all, give power to them. So, whether it is your extra twenty pounds, inabilities to perform certain physical feats, failure in relationships, or lack of income, realize that these things are happening because a change is necessary. Do not focus and feed the outcome, but rather open to the change being presented to you.

CHANGE>>>>>STRESS>>>>>LIMITATION>>>>>FEAR

There is a sequence in which fear is created and distributed in our lives, and this sequence originates with change. We are all creatures of habit and comfort. We will do whatever possible to develop a routine in which we feel safe, wanted, protected, and in charge. Once we establish this comfort zone, we do not wish to be altered, or forced to change. Changes in our lives lead into having to do something differently. Once we have established our norms and comfortable level of existence, creating a change brings about a sense of imbalance, especially since change usually leads into having to do something new. Any new activity will usually create a level of stress, because, going back to self judgement, which we spoke about earlier, we need to be perfect. We are also self taught and taught by society to act a certain way, speak a certain way, dress accordingly, and get involved in certain societal rituals. As the tribal creatures we are, when we are placed in a situation where we have to perform a new feat where others will judge us, we begin to add stress into the picture. You add to this the fact, that we do not want the new feat to change or disrupt our comfort zone, and now stress grows even more. As we venture into this new change and the stress continues to accumulate, we are forced to see and deal with our limitations. Thus, as these limitations are exposed, and we realize we have certain weaknesses, we are taken directly into the wonderful world of fear.

Our Guardian angels sometimes find it hard to believe how much energy and power we give to our fears. They also can't believe how much energy and effort we place in trying to hide our fears. Let me share the first of many situations that will be discussed in this book regarding conversations between my clients and their Guardian angels.

A woman in her late fifties came to see me for a reading because her husband had recently passed away. Besides trying to deal with her grief, she also felt paralyzed and unable to move on with her life by herself. She told me that for two months after her husband's death, she prayed to God every day, and asked that she be given the strength to move on and deal with all the new responsibilities presented to her. Her husband always handled the finances, took care of all the home repairs, to the point that she never even bothered to learn how to drive.

Her Guardian angel advised her that she still had many years ahead, and that she had the free will to either remain frozen in her fear, or make steps to gain the knowledge which would assist her to provide for herself. The woman said she was better off dead than to attempt at her age to learn new things just to survive in solitude. Her angel explained that her husband's soul was in transition and that he was in a situation similar to hers. He was afraid to move to the next level, leaving her alone, and unable to function in her life. So now, due to fear, she was stuck in her physical life and her husband was stuck in the spiritual realm. Her angel told her she was never alone, if she could start to let go of her fears, he would bring assistance in all the areas of her life. In return, her husband would also lose his fear, enter the spirit level with ease, and she would have the resources to gain back things in her life she felt had been lost. One of those things was to reconnect with her children and grandchildren, who had become strangers over the last ten years. Her angel proceeded to ask her what her biggest fears were at this very moment. My client responded by saying that she was not able to handle the financial mess her husband had left behind, was not able to go anywhere unless someone drove her, and the overwhelming sense of loneliness she felt did not allow her to move forward. Her angel than reminded her of the following memories regarding her current life.

She was told how at the age of seventeen, her father wanted to teach her how to drive, and how she was so eager to learn, but her mother did not feel this was safe. Her mother also believed women in general did not belong behind the wheel of a car, and further discouraged her from driving. Again at twenty-one, the year she met her husband, he had an extra car in the garage which he offered to fix and give to her. He had offered to teach her to drive, but she said no, because she enjoyed the idea of having him drive her places. When her daughter gave birth to her first grandchild, her husband again wanted to teach her to drive, in case any emergency might arise. Her husband thought that if she drove, she would be able to help her daughter or granddaughter if anything went wrong and he was not accessible. Again she said no, she was afraid that if an emergency did come up, she would be so nervous driving she might have an accident. Her angel said, "Three times we placed an opportunity for you to learn to drive, so that when this situation came up now, you would have one less thing to worry about." "The first time, you feared what your mother and society would think of you driving when most women at that time did not." " The second time, you feared that if your husband did not constantly chaperone you he would lose interest in you." " Finally, the third time, you feared that you would be an inadequate driver and be useless in a stressful situation."

Fear had stopped this woman from a simple lesson, and this same fear also froze her from handling finances, and developing a larger field of friends which now created this empty void in her life. Her angel went ahead and continued explaining all the other things in her life she walked away from , which would have made this transition a bit easier. The woman cried and truly understood all the times fear entered her life and did not allow her to progress. She assumed her husband would always be there and there was no need to release those fears. Her Guardian angel also mentioned future events and situations, which would be placed in her path to give her another chance to gain control of her life. This same woman called me almost two years later from her cell phone while driving her grandchildren to the park. And by the way, she was driving a new car she paid for with money she invested, after taking a class at the Community College with some new friends.

From this story we can see how the anticipation of a fear, which has no real value or power, can stop us from gaining various levels of experiences. We tend to live in a world where we are afraid to let go, attempt new things, move to new areas, or even discover a well-hidden talent. Just the idea of having to deal with changes, stress, and our individual limitations, once again, pushes us into the world of fear. We struggle in our existence and lose out on so many wonderful new events, possibilities, and levels of love when we give in to our fears.

Another area of fear, which our angels claim we place too much emphasis on, is the fear of death. Obviously, no one looks forward to this event, but eventually, it will be part of our human experience. Our Guardians find it amusing how we try to amass as many material things in life, when in actuality, we are here to amass experiences, emotions, and love. None of those three things can be borrowed, purchased, or taken from another person. As we get older, we focus on death as the next big chapter waiting for us. The idea of death has already been explained in many books and articles as a transition, not an ending. Yet, the idea that it will eventually knock on our door, makes us think that we need to gain as much as possible in the material world before it actually arrives. We are so afraid to let go of this life, thinking it is the only one we will ever know, that sometimes we are afraid to open to positive changes because, we don't want to let go of old patterns, which we feel will never be available to us again.

The fear of death plays out in our lives in two ways. One, is the fear of our own individual death, and the other, is the fear of the death of someone we love. Many elderly individuals, who are closer to death than to physical life, cling to life support machines longer than necessary due to this fear. Our angels tell us that we are physical, mental, emotional, and spiritual beings. The physical part of our makeup only knows one thing, and that is to survive as long as possible. Once we cease to exist physically, our body will not get a second chance to spring back into action. Because of this, and the internal fear of death, a person will lay comatose in a hospital for years refusing to let go of their physical existence. Every physical cell of that body refuses to let go. Once the individual begins to listen to it's own spiritual body, which is telling it that it is Ok to let go, than the physical body begins to shut down.

As we mentioned before, unknowing changes create stress, and one of the biggest unknown events in our society is death. Yes, we have thousands of documented cases of near death experiences in which we have been given a preview of the next stage, but that barely touches the surface of the millions of people who have never heard of them or simply refuse to believe in them. The worse case scenario of this fear is that once the inevitable death occurs, this fear can be strong enough to prevent the soul from moving forward into the spiritual realm as in the case of my client's husband mentioned earlier. This fear will not allow the soul to enter the transition in its original sense of beauty and tranquility. Our guardian protectors want us to know that death is basically a way of calling time out, getting our perspectives in order, and than trying again with an improved game plan. Death will never be an end to our existence, and once it gets close to our vicinity, we need to allow it to proceed. We need to do this for ourselves and for others as well. Our spirits will live on, and we do not lose the love, memories, and wonderful experiences we have gathered. This same idea applies to the loss of a loved one. One of the worst things we can do is refuse to let someone go when they have reached their moment of transition. The departed soul can hear us when we cry and scream out that we don't want them to leave. This makes it difficult for them to release their hold on the physical plane and some of these souls, which I refer to as lost souls, can be stuck in this level for hundreds of years.

Let me share another example of how fear can be so destructive in our lives. A gentleman in his early thirties came to see me one afternoon for a reading. He was basically urged by his wife who had already seen me a few weeks earlier. He was married for eight years, had a good job, was very happy with his wife, but felt incomplete because they were not enjoying a healthy sex life, and were not able to have children. He and his wife had been to various doctors and therapists to make sure there were no physical or emotional problems creating this situation. Physically there was no reason for them not to have children and the therapy seemed to reveal no deep emotional scars on either of their psyche.

During his reading, his Guardian angel showed me a glimpse of his past life. He was once a woman, living in Europe, in the early 1800's. At the age of twenty she was in charge of a group of children whose parents had been killed in war. This temporary shelter where she worked served as an orphanage for these children. The place was very crowded and dirty, and this temporary job eventually became a full time responsibility for her. After a few years of caring for these children, she became exhausted of caring for children that were not even hers, and began wondering if she would ever have any of her own. Her dedication to these orphans took away any kind of social life she might have. She decided to walk away from this job, concentrate on her own personal life, and maybe start her own family. After three years of unsuccessful courtships and no marriage proposals, she began to think that no man would ever marry her and she would never have her own children. This thought eventually grew into an obsession and in turn evolved into a powerful fear. As the years continued to pass, she was so afraid of not finding a husband and having children she decided to marry a man she did not love. She just wanted someone that would give her a chance at becoming a mother. Right after her marriage, she discovered that the orphanage had been shut down. Even though this made her a bit sad, she was focused on the idea that soon she would be raising her own children.

After two years of attempts she was not able to become pregnant, and during her third year of marriage her husband had a massive heart attack and lost his life. Barely, thirty years old, she now felt abandoned and too old to remarry. She truly missed her work with the children at the orphanage and began entering a heavy state of depression. This became so bad that she stopped eating, did not properly take care of herself, thus developing a serious intestinal problem which took her life a year later. At the end of this reading I asked this man what was his biggest worry in relation to his sexual intimacy with his wife. He stated that the idea of not being a father made him inferior and less of man. He was afraid that by continuing to make love to his wife, and not get her pregnant, he was simply adding to her sadness. He also shared that he had an underlying fear of getting old, being alone, or his wife dying before him, leaving him by himself. I personally felt he was taking all of this to an extreme, especially visualizing himself with no children, old, and dying by himself when he was in his early thirties!

The man's Guardian angel stated that the fear of his past life, in regards to dying without having a family, had carried over into this life. Even though physically, his sperm count was in the normal range, each cell of his body was holding the emotions and fear of his past life. Without consciously being aware, his body had received the message from his past life that he would never have children and was destined to be lonely. Obviously, this was the outcome of his past life, but his body carried enough emotional ammunition to bring this message forward.

Out of curiosity, I asked him how long had he carried this fear with him. He looked down at the floor, slowly lifted his head, and said as far back as he could remember. So, before he was married, he had already established an underlying fear that he would not have any children and be lonely throughout his life.

Understanding where this fear originated, gave this man a new sense of hope, and anticipation for future positive changes. His angel went on to explain that our minds are so powerful, once we realize where the origin of the problem comes from, it starts releasing the hold it has in our life. It will not matter if it is a physical, emotional, or spiritual hold, the mind will understand that the origin no longer applies to the present life, and begin to ignore that fear. This man left my office saying that for the first time, since he was married, he finally realized that every time he was making love to his wife, he was afraid that he would never give her a family. He was also afraid that eventually she would find someone else and leave him. The actual sex act had become a mission or responsibility, and not an act of enjoyment which forced him to want it less and less in his marriage. He smiled as he left my office and said, "Thanks to my Angel, I can accept what happened in the past, and this fear no longer has to be part of my current life."

Again we see how a strong negative aspect of fear, this one coming from a past life, can eventually block us from moving forward and accomplishing our life missions. With this in mind, we need to realize that as we confront fear issues in our lives, we need to make sure they are totally resolved. We do not want to hamper our ability to fulfill our life mission by carrying excess fear from a past life. I try to tell individuals in my classes and workshops that we need to truly understand difficult issues in our lives, such as a divorce, a chronic illness, death in the family, or a financial disaster. We need to learn to overcome the issue, step away from it, no matter how much time and effort we spend to do so.

We do have control over our fears for they have been created by us. A fear does not exist unless it has already been experienced, in this lifetime or a past one. We need to go out of our way to find the origin of our fears, and release the hold they have created in our lives. We also have to understand that sometimes fear is just our defense mechanism for not wanting to deal with a change in our life. Knowing that change will be a constant pattern in our life, we should be willing to bend, twist, and adapt to the new roads laid out in front of us. Realizing that many of these changes are being placed in front of us by our Guardian angel for our best and highest good, will also ease some of the stress. Look at changes like swinging doors, which can take us to a new level if we pass through them, or allow something positive from the outside to enter our lives. If we start looking at fear as a chance for growth, maybe we can gain better clarity as to who we are, and what we are attempting to accomplish in this life. Our Guardian angels would never create a change which is meant to harm us or push us away from our goals, but rather to assist us in our journey and allow us to give fear less credence.

Visual/Mental Exercise for dealing with unwanted or upcoming fears:

The mind is extremely powerful but can be fooled very easily. The next time a negative event or situation comes into your life, take a moment to experience it first. Instead of dealing with the stress of the event and the possible changes it might bring, simply play out the event entirely in your mind. Allow your mind to experience all the possible outcomes first before it plays out in your real life. This means running the event in as much detail as you can through your mind with use of your imagination and visualization. Run it several times, until the mind begins to accept is as a memory or something you have already done. By doing this you are programming the mind to be conditioned for the event. When the event actually arrives, mentally you are better prepared and the stress level normally produced will be reduced dramatically.

For example, if you suspect or have been told that your current employment is about to be terminated, see yourself in a better working situation in or out of the company you are in.

Experience, feel, and see all the positive outcomes created by this change in your life. Our mind, according to our angels, is the most efficient tool to recreate our future. Most of us are too busy worried about the fears instead of programming the changes we wish to encounter. Visualization is a powerful form of bringing things we want in our lives or removing those we are not happy with. I have used this tool many times throughout my life, and it has proven to be very effective.

Once I was told I had a small tumor growing very close to my spine and surgery would be very risky. For two weeks I imagined the tumor shrinking. I visualized a hammer smashing the tumor into small pieces, or else I would send little soldiers with machine guns to destroy it. Three weeks after being told about the tumor, I returned to the hospital for x-rays, and no sign of the tumor could be found. When I first entered college, I had no means of personal transportation, and depended on buses to get me back and forth from my home. On several occasions, while riding the bus, I had a vision of myself stepping off on the second bus stop, and being attacked by a homeless man with a knife. The first couple of times I had this vision it really scared me, and I would find myself sitting in the bus drenched in sweat. After four or five reviews of this same scene, I just taught myself to observe it but not become emotionally attached to it. Two months later, late at night, the vision played out in my real life as reality. Having seen the vision over and over in my mind prepared me for the actual attack. I was able to kick the homeless man and run to the next oncoming bus, and make it home safely. Again, by viewing the scene first in my mind I was better equipped to handle the stressful event. My Guardian angel had prepared me for the event, which in turn possibly saved my life.

Let's give it a try!

Find a quiet comfortable place where no one will disrupt you for at least five minutes. With dim lighting, close your eyes, take three long deep breaths. Think of a situation in your life which is adding stress or creating fear. See, analyze, and examine the entire situation. Now, think of the outcome which you feel will be to the best and highest good for you, and anyone else involved in this situation. Use your imagination and start seeing the changes taking place to make this situation disappear. Feel the relief, feel the sense of worry leaving your mind and body, and see the positive outcome that awaits you. Doing this for approximately five minutes every other day for a few days, will not only remove much of the stress involved, but bring about the positive change much quicker into your life. Spend more time feeling the outcome of the positive change than focusing on the issue you are trying to release. Your body, mind, and spirit, will eventually focus more energy anticipating the positive change, and forget about the situation causing the fear or stress in your life.

Affirmations you can use to deal with issues of fear and changes:

(Affirmations are simply phrases and statements which we can say over and over to ourselves to reinforce positive ideals and create strengths in various parts of our lives.)

1. **All changes and incidents which are placed in my path are for my best and highest good.**

Or

2. **My Guardian angel brings changes to me in order to provide me with opportunities, which will assist me in accomplishing my life mission without fear.**

Chapter 4

Second Message: Acceptance

Our Guardian Angels feel that we, as humans, still need to work on the concept of acceptance. We tend to be caught up in a constant state of asking, that when opportunities arise for us to receive, we do not know how to handle it. Acceptance, according to our Guardian angels, is simply the ability to let destiny flow in divine manner. We have to learn to co-exist with the process of acceptance by being open to changes. Many of us, when we were in the spirit plane preparing to enter a new life on earth, were so anxious to come back and really make a difference in the world. We wanted to save lives, educate, teach, or heal the planet. We forgot that as individuals, we also have personal needs which need to be met in order to access and accomplish the life mission we created for ourselves. The situation that has been taking place is that in the last twenty or thirty years, so many souls are returning to heal and balance the planet, that their main intention is to give or provide. I have had so many clients come to see me for personal consultations with their Guardian Angels, armed with a list of questions and concerns about all the people they worry about, and nothing for themselves. This might seem like a very noble and selfless act, but it does not allow them to see the total picture of who they are, and what their role is with all the people they are worried about. They simply want to know about their family members, children, pets, and friends. They have all these worries about individuals around them, but no concern for their own self development or state of mind and spirit. They are consumed with the responsibility that they need to resolve and save the lives of all these people.

The sad thing is that many of these clients are people with incredible open hearts who want to help others, yet they themselves are hurting inside emotionally. They ignore their own issues by becoming consumed in other's problems. Financially, they are ruined because they need to use their money to help others in need. Energetically, they are exhausted and have no time for themselves. The worst part is that their ability to discover who they are and what makes them happy is put on hold. Now I am not saying that we shouldn't go out of our way for our fellow man, on the contrary, that is what we are here to do, but not to the point where we forget to accept as well. Our angels have told me that they are amused when certain individuals pray for a specific opportunity to open in their lives, yet when this opportunity arrives, they feel they cannot accept it because someone else might need it more than them. There is no universal penalty for asking and receiving; the penalty comes about when we have and refuse to share due to greed or prejudice behavior. Think about it, if you can attain more things in your life, the more abundance you have that you can share with others.

Many people are still living under the idea that to be a true spiritual being and loving person, you need to neglect material items and self sacrifice. This focus of Spiritual growth might work for a few Masters who come into our planet to serve as leaders or serve as examples, but it is not a requirement for Spiritual enlightenment. On one occasion, I had a client who left me a telephone message to please return her call so I could provide her with more detailed information of my services. I returned the call, explained what I did, and at the end of the conversation, I also told her what my fees were. At that moment she became insulted, said she had seen me on a television show, and felt I had some beautiful words of wisdom to share. Now that she realized I charged for my services, I was no longer a good role model. According to her, any true spiritual person does not charge, they simply serve God asking nothing in return!

Our Angels have told me over and over, abundance is given to all of us by God, it is our right to have what our hearts desire. When I told this woman that I also had bills and financial responsibilities to handle, she said, "A true spiritual person will live off the streets, be homeless if necessary, as long as they are serving God's mission." Before I could say another word she hung up the phone. Again, this false belief that we must sacrifice our existence to be pure of heart and soul is maintained in the minds of many, yet many who believe this will not give up all their worldly possessions to attain this level of spirit.

I myself, fell into this trap when I was first thinking about leaving my regular job as a manager for the local Telephone Company. I decided to accept my psychic and spiritual abilities, and open to the public and try to assist people with problems they had. I dedicated a few hours after work, and invited people to my house for a personal psychic reading. Upon finishing the reading, I felt so awkward asking a fee for the time I spent with them. Yes, I had spent an hour of my own time, yes I was giving them valuable information which would benefit their lives, and yes, at times after the readings I would also perform a healing to remove a physical pain or discomfort. Somehow, I felt that my ability to tap into this information was a gift from God and I was not supposed to charge a fee. Again, this was a very noble idea on my part, and at the beginning I would do these readings and healing sessions for free, but suddenly when I was receiving phone calls for ten to twenty appointments a week, my personal time was becoming less and less. I realized I was providing a service, and to charge for a service was perfectly normal. Even with that new concept, I still had a hard time, and used to charge only ten or fifteen dollars for all the work I did, and many times still sent some clients home with no charge. At other times, I asked for an optional offering from the clients because I still had my regular full time job providing me with a salary. I began to realize that something shifted whenever I did accept a payment for my services. When I was paid for the work I provided, I also felt a sense of acknowledgment from the client. It was almost as though by my accepting their payment, we had created a bond or energetic exchange, which allowed them to accept my work with gratitude of a different personal nature. In the past when I was not accepting payments, some of my clients were hurt, embarrassed, upset, and even said they would not come back again unless I accepted a payment for my time. I began to realize that this bond, this exchange, was essential for the session to be complete, even if it was a minimal payment. This brings us back to the topic of this chapter. Those clients who came to see me and actually received some life changing information could not just accept this and walk away. They felt it wasn't right if I did not charge them. Again, they could not simply accept something in their life with nothing in return. Some clients even told me that if I would not accept a payment, they wanted to know what they had to do for their Guardian angel in order to pay them back for the information they provided. Many times in the beginning, their angel would tell me to tell the person to simply give me a hug. This served a dual purpose.

One of the reasons was to allow the person to hug me, in representation of them hugging their Angel. The other reason, was they knew I had issues with acceptance, especially being hugged by strangers! This way, they could change my fear of being hugged, and also give the client a chance to return an embrace, as a form of compensation. I could have very easily omitted this request from their angel, but I knew that hug that I feared was an issue I had to overcome, and bottom line during that reading, I was working for the Guardian angel, and just couldn't refuse.

Another important aspect of acceptance, as told to me by our Guardian angels, is the limitations we place in accepting things. This theory is explained very simply in the words from the book, "Conversations with God", which I truly recommend to all. The author, Neal Donald Walsch, writes that we as human beings limit what we ask for when we pray to our God Source. For example, we find ourselves in a situation where we need five hundred dollars to resolve a problem. We ask in prayer of God and our angels to help us attain these five hundred dollars to remove this burden. Now remember, this person was short of cash to begin with before this unexpected financial problem arrived. This person would pray every night for God to give them the exact amount to resolve the problem. Why limit their request to just five hundred, why not one thousand or ten thousand? God's love for us is unconditional with no limitations. There is enough abundance and riches on this planet for everyone, but only a few who really push to attain it seem to receive it. We generally see God as a fearful parent, approaching him or her with caution whenever we need to ask for something. Again, as in the previous chapter, fear plays a role in our ability to accept things. Our angels reinforce the idea behind Donald Walsch's book by restating that all in the universe is in perfect communication. What this means is that if we are in the process of divine intervention, and have an unexpected amount of one thousand dollars coming our way, the fact that we are asking for five hundred only can alter or change the path of the original thousand. Always ask for the amount you need or whatever higher amount is available for you to keep that window of opportunity open. Another reason we are afraid to accept is the fact that by having more in our lives, this could lead to changes, which in turn leads to the fear factor once again. Generally speaking human beings are hesitant of changes, and accepting opportunities will eventually lead us to change one thing or another.

Let me introduce to you a client by the name of Michael. He was a businessman, approximately forty years of age who carried a huge burden throughout most of his life. He came to see me for a session with his Guardian angel to get some clarity in his life. It seems that his mother died when he was twenty two years old, and she requested a favor from him before her death. She asked Michael to please finish his college education and become a pharmacist like his father, to work with him side by side so that his father would not feel alone. Apparently, his mother had been diagnosed with incurable cancer. She knew her time was limited and her husband would be left alone. Michael agreed reluctantly, and after her death felt he was trapped living a life that was not his. He graduated, became a pharmacist, and for the last fifteen years was working by his father's side. The sad thing was that once he graduated and received his degree, within three years of working as a pharmacist, he realized it was not what he wanted to do all his life. Feeling obligated to his mother, Michael basically put his personal feelings on hold, as well as his life, and continued in a profession which was destroying him emotionally. Many times after work he would assist his elderly father with household chores, stay over his father's house, have dinner, and make sure he wasn't lonely. What he did not know, until his angel informed him, was that his father was also asked for the same favor by his mother. It seemed his mother asked her husband to make sure their son finished his studies, to stay close to him, and to make sure he was not alone. His father, just like Michael, had lost the desire to keep working at the pharmacy but stayed to honor his wife's request. Both Michael and his father had been given so many chances to accept changes in their lives and careers, but turned them down to honor their beloved. In the meantime, they wasted many years of possible changes, which would have enriched their lives more than staying working together at the pharmacy. Our angels want us to know that they are responsible for creating new doors, passages, and opening new adventures, but we have to learn to accept things in our lives and not hold back due to fear, insecurity, or in Michael's case, feeling guilty if he did not honor his dying mother's wishes.

In order to accept things in our lives we must learn to truly believe that we deserve the very best. Society, family ideas and upbringing, and our own self esteem play a very important role in our ability to accept richness and positive flow of outcomes on a daily basis. Once we begin to tell ourselves that we are not good enough, or we take other people's negative beliefs of who we are as reality, we push away our natural ability to accept from others or life in general.

I recall a movie I saw once, in which an old homeless man found sleeping in the alley was taken in by a caring family. He hesitantly agreed to stay at the family's home. He was forced to wash, dress in new clothes, comb his hair, learn to eat with proper manners at the dinner table, and was being scheduled to regain a connection with society. After one week of these new changes, the old man couldn't take it anymore, got his old clothes back from the box he was told to put them in, and returned to living in the streets. He had accepted his role as a homeless person and developed a sense of self comfort in an atmosphere where he was in charge of his life, even though many would think he was in total neglect. It turned out he was not loved by his parents, was made fun of in school when he was young because he stuttered, and a business and family failure by the age of forty had pushed him away from society, thinking he deserved nothing better. In his situation, he could not accept any improvement in his life because he was stamped a failure by his family, school, and work environment.

We do not need to be in a level of failure or poverty because we have been condemned or labeled in a negative form by others. We should always feel that we have the right to receive positive things in our lives. Our world and our bodies are a constant exchange of energy. From the moment we awaken, make decisions throughout the day, and end our day, we are in a constant flurry of exchange of energies with others and with our planet. Our angels want us to realize that in that exchange of energies, many opportunities are being created for us to accept and connect with the accomplishment of our life mission. The same way we hold the idea of giving to be sacred and honorable, we must also hold the idea of accepting in the same category. Many of us will not think twice at the idea of giving something away, but when someone shows up at our doorstep with an opportunity, we step back to analyze and question rather than to receive quickly. We need to accept this flow of positive changes which they provide to us, regardless of whether it comes in a form of monetary gain, notability, or personal achievement.

Remember, your ability to accept from others and from life, is your acknowledgment that you are a being of spiritual love and deserve abundance. In accepting this abundance, you accept to be loved in all aspects of your being, which in turn, allows you to live within your perfection.

Many times when I have been doing a presentation, lecture, or workshop, I would select someone from the audience to participate in an exchange with their angel as a demonstration. To relieve the stress of me picking one particular person from an eager group, the angels would place a bright round light over the head of the individual that they wanted me to choose. The amazing thing was that after the lecture was over, many of the individuals chosen would approach me and ask why were they chosen or selected from such a large group. They actually had a hard time accepting that they were worthy, or special enough to be chosen by the angels to receive an answer or insight to an issue in their lives. We need to allow our lives, to be ones in which we truly balance our ability to give to others, while recognizing that we also deserve to accept from others, especially when they want to give us something from their own free will with love. In this even exchange of energy, we truly can appreciate the beauty which spirit provides in creating harmony, peace, and love. As final words to this chapter of acceptance, I wish to state the three basic fundamentals of acceptance.

1. Accept things in life, because nothing is ever coincidence or happens by accident.
2. In your acceptance, be ready to give back as well.
3. When you accept changes with the intent that it will be for your best and highest good, you have started the steps of your personal and spiritual evolution.

Meditation to assist you in the process of acceptance:

All meditations provided in this book require a few simple guidelines. Find a quiet location where you will not be interrupted for at least fifteen minutes. Dress comfortably with no tight restrictions around the waist or feet. Get in a relaxed position with your spine upright, not laying flat, because you will give your body an excuse to fall asleep. Have dim to low lighting around you. You may add other elements which might enhance your level of relaxation such as incense, soft music, aroma therapy, or the sounds of a fountain in the background.

Close your eyes and take three deep breaths, holding each for a count of five before you release. With each breath you connect with your mind, body, and spirit, allowing the air you release to exit slowly. Repeat this process three times with each sequence allowing your body to relax deeper and deeper. Clear your mind of any random thoughts, or if possible, just let them run through your mind but do not give them any attention. Do not get into an argument with your thoughts, you will always lose because your ego does not want you to have a free flowing open mind.

Once you finish your breathing patterns, begin focusing on an area of your life which you feel is lacking. This may be money, love, spirituality, or any other part of your life you wish to enhance. Now, see yourself standing on a stage and the audience is standing and applauding. Realize you have been chosen as the grand prize winner, and everyone is genuinely happy for you.

Hear the clapping throughout the full theater, feel the joy omitted from the crowd towards you, and most of all feel the excitement of knowing you will soon be awarded. At this point, imagine a large curtain behind you opens, and finally you get to see your grand prize. You are told that all you need to do is walk over to the computer right next to you and type exactly what you want this grand prize to be. There are no limitations and, you deserve to have whatever makes you happy and complete. You finish typing your request, and instantly as you type your last word and press the button, the curtain opens completely. All you need to do is turn around and accept your reward. See yourself walking closer and closer towards your prize with your arms extended in total acceptance. Acknowledge the gratitude for having this prize given to you, and know many other things will be given to you throughout your life. Enjoy this process of acceptance and the feelings associated with it. Allow your mind, body, and soul to connect with this wonderful feeling of acceptance. Allow yourself to feel comfortable as this gift or prize is now part of your life.

Next, see yourself thanking the audience for choosing you as the recipient of this wonderful prize. You may bow, wave, or simply throw them a kiss. Allow the curtain to close, keeping your gift safe until you decide to use it. See the audience begin to exit the theater, but hold on to the feeling of acceptance. Allow the lights to dim on the stage and slowly breathe in three times, with each breath you hold the energy of acceptance deeper in your soul. Allow the vision to slowly disappear as you return to your awakened state of consciousness. Before you open your eyes, know that you are willing to accept more in your life from this moment on. You will not have any fear or hesitation. Take one final deep breath, and when finished, slowly open your eyes and hold on to that wonderful experience throughout the remainder of the day.

Chapter 5

Third Message: Health

Health is a topic which our Guardian angels focus upon in great detail. Almost ninety percent of the time when I am doing a reading with a client and their angel, the angel takes some time to discuss certain health issues, and the origins creating these issues. Our angels feel that we are struggling at an enormous level just to maintain a healthy body. They want us to understand various factors of our day to day functioning which affect how our body responds. The angels also want us to understand that we do indeed have a great deal of control of how our body can be maintained at a high optimum level. More importantly, they want us to understand that we need to become more sensitive to communication, which our bodies provide to us. We have a great deal of control when it comes to the breakdown and maintenance of both the inside and outside structures of our physical makeup. In this chapter we will discuss health in three categories which all have a direct relationship to the physical body. These three elements are the emotional, energetic, and spiritual sub-bodies, which react directly with the physical body.

Emotional Element

One of the greatest differences between humans and other life forms is our vast level of emotions. We have such a wide variety of emotions which change daily. The first thing we need to focus upon, according to the angels, is that we constantly co-exist in three dimensions which are commonly known as body, mind, and spirit. Ironically, the Catholic church, also holds a similar theory in the Holy Trinity. The church uses the division of Father, Son, and Holy Spirit or Holy ghost. These three elements are represented by God, the son Jesus, and the Holy Spirit symbolically seen as a white dove. The angels inform me that our physical body is the God Source of who we are in a material essence, the son Jesus, represents our mental body which is an extension of the thoughts of God, and finally the Holy Spirit or Dove, is our divine Spiritual body which is our everlasting vessel.

The body deals with the physical nature and structure of the material which holds us together in functional capacity. This consists of our organs, skeleton, muscles, brain, tissues, and all other physical elements contained within. Our mind consists of our thoughts, ideas, emotions, feelings, and reasoning capacities. The third component, our spirit, allows us to connect with faith, inner belief, life purpose, and is also our never-ending connection to our God Source. Our angels say that whenever we create an emotional imbalance it will eventually lead to an imbalance in our physical well being. An individual who is emotionally distraught will force the physical body to work harder by creating unwanted anxiety and stress. This will in turn, force the body to slow down, and bring about issues such as fear, insecurities, and depression. All our organs and body parts have responsibilities and direct communication with different emotions in our lives. This information is nothing new, authors such as Carolyn Myss, have written many books about the interaction of body and feelings. Unfortunately, only fifteen to twenty percent of our population has bothered to read these books or even consider the possibilities of doing their own research into their health issues. The individual becomes accustomed to running to a doctor for a quick cure without first analyzing why the problem even originated.

We live in a fast pace world where we need to function at all costs without anytime available for self evaluations.

A few examples of body and emotion connections consist of financial worries and concerns with lower back pains. Sensitive and emotionally weak people who cannot handle changes or stress easily will force the stomach and intestinal area to weaken. Fear, the number one negative emotion, can effect any part of the body, but many times settles in the kidneys and circulation. A person who is afraid of seeing an obvious change in their life, eventually can be set back with eye difficulties such as visual weakness, nerve damage around the eyes, or even closed or weak water ducts. An individual who is afraid to step forward in a difficult situation can create problems with their circulation, ankles and feet. Other individuals who feel they never had any support in their lives can manifest physical ailments in the knees and shoulders. All organs in our bodies will have some type of direct reaction to all emotions and feelings that we express or fail to express. Difficult or negative issues which you confront on a daily basis, if left unattended for a long period of time, will begin to send messages with the part of the party it best associates with. Louise Hay's book, "You Can Heal Yourself", is a wonderful source of information which provides us with many physical ailments and their emotional counterparts.

According to our Guardian angels, you are in direct command of your three counterparts, body, mind, and spirit. The physical body is the final resting place for the unbalanced energy which has been thrown around in the other energetic fields such as the emotional and mental bodies.

Since the physical body is the place where we feel the final outcome, which is pain and discomfort, this is usually the only body we eventually go out of our way to try and fix. Sadly, once we feel this has been fixed, we ignore all the symptoms which led to the breakdown, and end up repeating the same patterns over and over. Finally, modern traditional medicine is looking into these areas of origin in order to stop the repetitive patterns from returning to the body.

An example which comes to mind in relation to this topic of physical problems is a case of a young woman around the age of thirty two. She set up an appointment to see me for a reading because she had horrible stomach pains for three years, and no medical tests performed could detect the cause of these pains. She had visited various medical professionals with different specialities, had taken countless medications, and never had found a relief for her pain. As a natural healer and practitioner of Reiki Healing, which is a form of energetic hands on healing, my approach was for a healing session rather than a reading. I felt we needed to clear any blockages in her physical structure which was causing this pain. In Reiki healing, regardless of where the pain is located, the entire body is worked upon to create an overall sense of balance from head to feet. Upon reaching the area of her stomach I felt a sensation of cold air emitting upward from the mid-central portion. As I focused on this area to send healing energy she began to shed some tears. Now, you have to take into consideration that many areas of healing in Reiki do not even require physical touch. I knew I wasn't touching or pressing against her stomach to create further pain, but to make sure I asked her if what I was doing was aggravating the situation more. She responded no, she was not in any worse pain, and asked that I continue to do the healing.

As I focused again to send more healing energy, her sobbing began to become a bit more intense. Once again, I asked if she was okay, and again, in between her crying, she simply asked for me to please continue. As she continued to increase her sobbing, I finally decided to stop and get some insight as to why this energy was making her cry more and more. I asked if she could please share with me what she was thinking or feeling, which was making her cry so much. I felt uncomfortable proceeding with the healing until I could resolve the crying episodes.

It seemed that the moment I began to work over her stomach, which was her area of pain, she began to have visual flashbacks of a scene in her life that had occurred four years earlier.

I asked her if she felt comfortable sharing this with me. She began to tell me that four years ago she went through a very difficult divorce which had become more emotionally and physically draining with each day that passed. Adding to the stress was the fact that she was six months pregnant, and her husband had become physically abusive towards her. One night he was in such a rage that he hit her several times, threw her against the kitchen wall, and left the house. The beating she sustained caused her to have internal bleeding, she was eventually rushed to the hospital by a neighbor, where she eventually lost the child. I asked her what she did after leaving the hospital, and she responded by telling me that she called the police, her husband was arrested, and was not permitted back into the house due to a restraining order that was granted to her. She said the judge granted her the divorce within a few months. I told her I did not want to know what eventually happened when she came out of the hospital, I wanted to know what she actually did when she came home on an emotional level. She stayed quiet for a few moments, and then told me she remembered coming home, going to her bedroom, sitting on the floor while holding onto her stomach and crying for two days straight. She said all she could think about was how much she hated her husband, and how he caused her to lose their child.

During those two days, she only stepped away from the floor to go to the bathroom, never ate, or slept in her bed. As she continued to cry and share this experience with me I noticed the coldness coming from her stomach was starting to change. A warm energy was slowly taking it's place. She stopped crying after a few more minutes while I finished the Reiki healing session, and then I asked her to please sit up from the massage table and stand up.

This woman slowly lifted herself from the table, stood up a bit unbalanced, but with a smile on her face. She told me she felt something had shifted, and before I could ask another question, she began to stretch all about, bend down to touch the floor with her finger tips, and jump up and down. She looked at me with an incredible glow in her eyes and told me her pain was gone! You see, this was short of a miracle, the pain she had was a constant day to day, minute by minute pain, which had not changed at all throughout the three years. I followed up with this client one month later and than three months later. Her pain never returned.

What had happened was that she took the emotional setback of losing her child and being beaten, and placed that negative trauma experience in her stomach. When she sat on her bedroom floor for two days crying and holding her stomach, she focused all her anguish directly into that particular area of her body. On a conscious level, even though it took about a year, she felt she had conquered the trauma, meanwhile it was still repeating over and over in her emotional body in the area of the stomach. Eventually, this unresolved issue manifested as a pain in the same location which was not visible by medical tests, x-rays, or diagnostic procedures. The reason was that it had no physical cause or origin, it was emotional. The amazing thing about these physical and emotional ties is that they can occur from one lifetime to another. An unresolved issue from a past life could come back to haunt you in a physical manifestation in your present life. I worked for many years with a business associate, who as a hypnotherapist, resolved many physical traumas by doing regression work to past lives. Having the client relive the event in which these emotional blockages originated provided a safe environment for the conscious mind to understand, release, and heal. In many readings that I do, the Guardian angel will show me some scenes of the client's past life to assist them in blockages they presently have today.

Energetic Element

Our Guardian angels want us to understand that we need to look at everything in life as an energetic component. The second element which relates to our health places us in an energetic force field. We consist of various energies and vibrations wrapped around the inside and outside of this shell we call the human body. We have many bodies working together to form the one we see and feel physically. These layers of outside energy bodies all play a role in our overall health. When we are stricken with a physical illness, this illness has already penetrated these outside bodies, before actually settling into the physical.

We have an emotional body, which is constantly being tested on a daily basis as we deal with day to day experiences. We have an astral body which is an etheric extension of the physical body. This astral body is capable of wandering off in exploration while we sleep. It is responsible for assisting us in releasing fear and anxiety by playing out certain scenes in our dream state, as well as, going out to different dimension to find answers to questions that we consciously keep revolving in our minds. In addition to our physical, emotional, and astral, we also have the mental and spiritual bodies which together compose the human being. The mental body, according to our angels, works overtime recording and evaluating all our fears, doubts, questions, and everyday encounters. The differences between the emotional and mental bodies is that the mental body is a processing mechanism, while the emotional is strictly feelings. Finally, the spiritual body is our never ending soul connection to the God Source which continues evolving from lifetime to lifetime. All five of these bodies need to be in harmony in order for us to exist in perfect health. An entire book can be written about the functions and connections of these five bodies, but for this chapter I simply wish to introduce them briefly so you, the reader can know of their existence in relations to our health.

Our angels feel that we need to develop a stronger sensitivity to all aspects of our lives. The moment we feel something is off balance, we need to ask ourselves questions and investigate. By ignoring our emotions, fears, insecurities, and the inability to accept changes in our lives, we allow a negative energy to tear into one of our five body types. This tear will eventually turn into a physical problem. Viruses and infections are the end result of a breakdown in our various bodies, yet we see them as origins for illnesses.

In reference to the mental body, we are told by our angelic helpers that we fail to realize the unlimited potential of our minds in both a positive and negative manner. Our thoughts are actually vibrations which have potential for creating outcomes. Many times our own thoughts open the doors to negative health conditions. For example, let's say you arrive to work and notice that your co-worker has a horrible cold. If you spend the day thinking about the possibility that their cold will be transferred to you, then congratulate yourself the next morning when you wake up with a stuffy nose. The mind is so powerful that it will attempt to manifest what your thoughts carry.

The moment you tell yourself that your co-worker's cold will be passed to you, you have set off a direct command, which the mind will attempt to carry out. On the other hand, if you tell your mind that your immune system is strong and the cold will not enter your body, you actually create a protective shield which will dramatically reduce the odds of you getting the cold.

This same idea applies to someone who hates their job. As soon as they get up in the morning, they focus on how their job is so horrible, how it gives them a headache by just being there. The mind, as this person dresses and prepares for work, has been given a direct command.

Within a few minutes of arriving at their job, they find themselves with a pounding headache. Again, they blame the job atmosphere for this headache, rather than the two hours they spent beforehand predicting it. Our angels want us to be careful with the negative statements, thoughts, and ideas that we create, especially in relation to stress, anger, disappointment, jealousy, envy, and other areas which drain us mentally.

Taking the idea of energy transference one step further. The vibrations created on our thoughts cannot only hurt us, but bring negative complications to others as well. The same way that I, as a psychic, can use positive mental capabilities to heal, see angels, or provide insights to others, someone can also use their mental abilities to bring harm and destruction. This can be done unknowingly or at times willingly. Energetic thoughts when focused and processed over and over will gain strength. This means that negative thoughts, when created and given intent, will eventually have to be released in one form or another. This release will be upon yourself or the person you are focusing on. This release, once again, can be transformed as a health issue for yourself or the other individual.

An example of how this negative thought pattern works is as follows. If you have someone in your life that annoys you, and you are forced to deal with this person on a regular basis, you begin to develop a sense of dislike or even hatred towards this individual. Even though these thoughts are inside your mind and not spoken out loud, as vibrations, they are released into the universe. Due to the fact that these negative thoughts are intended for a particular individual, these vibrations will eventually be directed towards that person. Now, if that certain individual is a strong willed balanced person, these negative vibrational thoughts will simply bounce off their energetic bodies and crumble. On the other hand, if that individual is weak minded and susceptible to being influenced easily, these energetic thought vibrations can penetrate through all their body components and work themselves into a health problem or negative experience.

I once had a client come to see me, a young man in his early thirties, who was extremely worried about his mother. She had a difficult life and seemed to be withdrawn and very unsociable. His Guardian angel explained and pointed out various health problems which had arisen in his mother's life over the last six months. The young man was astonished at the angel's accuracy of all the ailments which his mother was suffering from. At the end, his angel advised him that his mother was the type of person to keep everything hidden inside, especially personal issues. She would not speak about her problems, resentments, old angers, or disappointments. The man shook his head in confirmation, and spoke about how his mother always kept all this inside and never smiled throughout much of her life. The angel continued, and stated that when an individual holds anger and negative memories inside without any form of release, this energy begins to build upon itself. If time continues to pass and this energy is not released or resolved, it reaches a boiling point where it explodes and begins to attack the physical body. My client was advised to find someone who could get his mother to speak and share memories of her life. She needed to release old patterns and fears that were locked inside her emotional body for many years. Her ability to release and share these thoughts were sufficient to reverse the process and start the baby steps towards physical healing. This is why I always tell people in my lectures or classes to try and deal with difficult issues in their lives such as deaths, divorces, or financial challenges, right from the start. Do not simply think about it when it happens. Take the time to analyze how these events have changed your life and make the effort to step away from them and seek the next path in your life mission. Holding on to these painful and difficult periods of our lives, we simply magnify them through time, and our physical bodies will pay the consequences sooner or later.

Spiritual Element

Finally, the third area of healing which I will discuss, is that of Spiritual health complications. The same way that a negative person can connect with fear, anger, or hatred, and mentally send that vibration to someone else, this same interaction can also be done by those in spirit. By spirit, I am referring to those who have died, and no longer exist in the physical plane.

Many people are under the notion that once a person connects with the death process, their emotional being and personality, along with everything connected to it is automatically transformed. On the contrary, a person who dies holding difficult emotional issues will still carry those issues or burden into the spirit state. By being removed from the physical body, they also have a higher sensitivity to those issues. This person, in the spirit state, can disrupt their own spiritual evolution, as well as, the physical state of someone they have contact with in the physical world.

It is extremely rare, but possible for someone to initiate an illness or physical problem because of a spiritual beings' energetic involvement. From the many cases of healings, spirit interventions, and possessions that I have encountered, only twice have I been called upon to perform a healing on someone whose source of physical complications were a direct manifestation from someone in spirit form. Nevertheless, I will address this in this chapter simply because it is possible. Our angels want us to understand that we are responsible for our actions and thoughts while in the physical body as well as the spiritual.

Many years ago I dealt with a man in his early fifties who had horrible leg pains, and medical doctors could not find any physical reasons for why he should have such pain in his right leg. They performed x-rays, scans, checked for muscular problems however, all tests came back negative. The pain came overnight and seemed to become more intense with each day that passed. I went to visit this man to see if I could offer some assistance. I tried my normal procedures of energy healing, I touched the area in question, and sent positive healing energy. Within a few minutes of doing this I could tell there was an outside interference. The hairs on the back of my neck stood up and I could feel a cold draft around the man's body. I then decided to raise my energy a bit higher to gain some clarity as to the origin of this strange feeling. Suddenly, I saw the spirit of an old man, standing right next to the man I was assisting. It was a man in his late sixties with a face of despair, fear, and a strong sense of being lost or confused. I eventually spotted a very important element of this spiritual vision I was receiving. This spirit was missing his right leg, the same leg which the man was complaining of intense pain. One thing that I have learned while working with those who cross over into the spiritual plane, is that once we cross over we no longer hold onto or experience physical pain. For this spirit to show itself to me missing a leg told me that they had not yet accepted their death.

It turned out that the spirit of this older man was stuck between the physical and spiritual realms. Two weeks prior, late in the evening, he was killed in a car accident. His leg was severed from the impact, and the loss of blood led to his death. Upon leaving his physical body, the first person he encountered was the man I was helping, who lived less than half a block from the scene of the accident. When I shared this information with my client, he had remembered that about two weeks ago, on his way home, he had seen a serious accident at the corner of his block. He also recalled seeing an ambulance and a couple of police cars, and thinking that the car was totally damaged. In fact, the next morning is was when his leg pain began. Apparently, the spirit of the man who was killed in the accident was in shock because it was an abrupt death, and he could not accept the fact he was dead. Even after the ambulance took his body away, his spirit remained in that area, and the first person he saw was this man coming home. He then followed him home seeking assistance. The spirit had attached himself emotionally to this man, and the pain that he endured physically before his death, was also attached to the energetic body of my client.

I was able to assist the spirit to understand his death and move forward in the process of entering the spiritual plane. This removed his emotional distraught from my client, and within five to ten minutes the pain that he was dealing with began to wear off. Within a fifteen minute span he no longer had any pain in his leg. Once again, this situation happens very rarely, so don't start thinking that the next time your doctor can't find a reason for a pain you are having that it means you have a spirit attached to you! We, humans have too many fears on this planet already without having to create new ones.

Our angels also advise us that in connection with all these elements which can harm the physical body, we also need to have common sense. We need to love ourselves enough to eat healthy, exercise, and deal with emotional instabilities in our lives. We need to balance our levels of stress, which unfortunately, is at an all time high since we crossed over to the year 2000. We need to let go of fear, addictive behaviors, start accepting life easier, and what it provides us on a daily basis We also need to heal our physical planet, it has been abused for so long. They also want us to find better ways of providing for humanity without constantly depleting nature, and destroying animal life, just to enhance our personal needs. We need to understand the communication within our five body types. Remember the sequence, when we are emotionally out of balance, our emotional body sends a message to the mental body. The mental body accepts this message and starts connecting with anger, depression, or solitude. It will then forward the message to the physical body where we begin to encounter health issues. We can intercept these messages before they get to the physical body to make the necessary changes in order to avoid health complications. Again, it is through understanding and accepting that we are more than the physical, and all of our other body types need to be recognized and respected as well.

Visual Exercise to Enhance our Health:

Just like the previous mental meditative exercise, place your body in a relaxed position, and breathe deeply three times. Each deep breath is to connect with the body, mind, and spirit.

Close your eyes and using all levels of your imagination, try to picture yourself in a beautiful mountain setting. It's a lovely sunny day with perfect temperature. Make the day as warm or as cold as you like. Imagine you just finished a short hike in the mountains and your body is ready for some rejuvenation. To your right, you see an opening in the mountain, close enough that you can walk to. This opening leads out to a rock ledge large enough to hold several people. From above the ledge you see a wonderful refreshing waterfall. Take your time in creating and seeing this image in your mind.

You can feel your body wanting to stand at this ledge and allow the waterfall to run over every inch of your existence. Go ahead and do just that, imagine yourself removing your back-pack, boots, and clothes. Under your clothes you can stay with a bathing suit that you have or if you feel daring, and considering there is no one else around for miles, you can simply remove all of your clothing. Don't wait, run over to this ledge, and start allowing this refreshing waterfall to run over your head and body.

As this water falls upon your body, imagine all negative thoughts which you have created, or thoughts that others have created and directed to you, be washed away with the force of the water. Any part of your body that is sore or tired instantly becomes stronger and more vibrant. Imagine this water hitting your skin, penetrating it, and entering your other energetic bodies. This water first cleanses all your organs and physical parts then, goes even deeper to cleanse your emotional, mental, astral, and finally your spiritual body as well. All negativity from your total body components are removed and revitalized. Feel your bodies take in this water and revive itself, feeling all negativity being removed and washed away. A sense of physical bliss takes over as you look around at the beautiful scenes of nature surrounding you. When you feel you have had enough, slowly walk away from the waterfall, simply lay out on the cool refreshing flat stone area, and allow the warm rays of the sun to dry you. Allow the sunshine to be the final cleansing and healing vibrations which touch your body. Stay here until you feel ready to stand up and continue on your journey. You are feeling vibrant, in charge of your life, and totally removed of all levels of negativity. Take three nice long deep breaths, open your eyes, and move forward with your wonderful day.

Chapter 6

Fourth Message: Focus

Remember as a child, whenever it was time to take an important test at school, we would take one of two approaches. Some of us would be up all night long for days studying and repeating all the possible questions and answers in our heads. Others would just ignore the stress, and maybe a few hours before the test read over some notes, while a few will just show up the day of the test, and just wing it. Our Guardian angels tell me that we in general, as humans, do the same thing in handling our day to day lives. We lack the ability to focus properly on our issues in life. The angels feel we have a tendency of stretching the duration of our problems due to our inability to see things differently, or failing not to take the total picture into consideration. They also feel we use the freeze and wait approach a little too often when obstacles are placed in our path. In this chapter, we will cover the meaning and process of focusing according to our spiritual helpers. Try to keep in the back of your mind, as you read this chapter, that our angels want us to realize that obstacles, and so called problems may actually be blessings or opportunities in disguise.

We are going to take two philosophies into consideration as I try to explain what our angels wish for us to understand when it comes to focusing. The first philosophy or understanding is that we all chose our life mission before we decided to incarnate upon this planet. Everyone of us took a great deal of time and planning to make sure we chose the essential experiences which our soul needed to further expand it's growth. This means that we all come here with a specific game plan or mission originated by us, which we plan to execute, and fulfill as much as possible, throughout the duration of our lives. It is not necessarily God's or the Source's mission for us, but rather, the mission in which we feel we need to experience as part of our journey, in order to make us more whole in the eventual reunion with our God.

Upon entering into our physical body, when we are born, the conscious recollection of the details we created for our life mission is pushed back into our subconscious mind. When we physically take our first breath and enter this world, we do not have this information readily available to us. This allows us to have a natural process of life where we are open to all emotions, possibilities, and experiences. Many of you disagree with this process and say that if we had a better idea as to what our life purpose is we wouldn't waste time and energy in other areas. This wasted time makes us feel non-productive leaving us feeling hopeless and lost. The answer I receive from our angels to this question is the following, " If we are born, knowing exactly what our life purpose was, we would not be able to properly accomplish it". Logically, this does not make sense! Doesn't it make sense that if you were born knowing you came here to be a firefighter and marry your high school sweetheart, you would avoid many mistakes and avoid lost time. Well, according to the angels, you would lose the main reason for returning to this planet, to have experiences. They say given the example above, you would mechanically graduate from high school, marry the only girl you dated, and train to be a firefighter. In this predetermined process, you would have lost the emotional reasoning behind making these decisions. In the real world, according to the angels, maybe as a teenager you witnessed a horrible fire across the street from your own home. You saw people screaming, crying, and desperation on the faces of all your neighbors. You saw the firefighters arrive, take control, save some lives, and the gratitude of those individuals fighting for their lives. You witnessed and experienced the gratitude of being responsible for helping others. That emotional experience created a stir in your soul which eventually, as an adult, made you want to be a part of that on a regular basis by becoming a firefighter. You felt the desperation of those people around you as a child and realized the value of life.

If you simply became a firefighter because you knew this was one of your life missions, you would do the work without the emotional value connected to it. Rather than a direct route to the finish line with little sense of self growth, compassion, learning, or interaction, you use your free will to gather the emotional power which leads you into fulfilling your life experience at the optimum level. Understanding this idea, we can allow ourselves to follow unexpected twists and turns in our lives, which are life changes placed by our angels. Sometimes these little obstacles that appear in our path are signals by our angels that we have gone off course, or that maybe we need to follow a new path. They are trying to align us with our life mission. Obviously, by also having this free will in our hands, we can also ignore these changes or destinations which are repeatedly placed in front of us, and delay or lose out on having these life mission experiences. Again, we are not created by God to be puppets, with no sense of having our own say in what we wish to experience. Our angels, with unconditional love, serve as our tour guides in life, taking us on voyages and experiences to aide us in accomplishing as much of our life mission as possible.

Now, I will briefly cover the second philosophy, before covering the actual focusing techniques that our angels wish for us to understand. This second philosophy which goes hand in hand with the first one, is the concept of destiny. Our angels say we need to open our minds to the idea that there are no coincidences, but rather a wonderful orchestrated series of events playing out daily in our lives. There is a divine sense of purpose in our daily activities, and we need to be attentive to new information and changes which confront us. People we meet, books that happen to fall into our hands, movies we attend, or invitations given to us, all serve as clues for us to gather, or place together like a puzzle to accomplish our life mission. There was a television program that aired a few years ago called, "Joan of Arcadia", it presented this idea with beautiful simplicity. A young high school girl who has contact with God in various human forms, is constantly asked to get involved in new projects with no idea of the outcomes. At the end, the outcomes serve as major learning lessons, for her and those around her. Destiny is basically a series of events, which your soul will have a magnetic pull towards, throughout your life, regardless of your conscious desire to avoid them. These events are very important issues you created for your life mission, and they carry more weight than others. You might avoid them for a few rounds, but eventually before the fight is over, you will get your knock out punch.

As we take these two philosophies and merge them into one, we begin to allow life to resonate in our hearts and souls with much less struggle. We begin to have more clarity in decisions we make, and allow ourselves to become participants in the dance of life. We no longer stay in the background wondering if we will ever cross over onto the dance floor. We start to become anxious in a positive manner when something new or challenging is presented to us. We no longer have to anticipate a change with a sense of fear or failure. Our angels tell us that by becoming open to new changes, we actually speed up the process of connecting with our life mission. Unfortunately, they also say that at this point of human existence, the average soul, upon physical death, is only accomplishing between fifty to sixty percent of their total life mission. These are not very good results.

Let us start understanding just how powerful we, as human beings actually are. The angels say God or the Source, created mankind to be co-creators. This is a gift most humans fail to accept or fail to use after opening. What this concepts states is that with the use of imagination and visualization, we can see and create solutions and changes in our minds thereby, transferring them into realities. Everything you think about is automatically energized, and once it becomes energized it then connects with intent and motion which forces it to be released into the universe. Our minds are responsible for creating our reality day by day, depending on the thoughts we manifest. As I mentioned in the health chapter, your ideas about illness can bring about, or prevent it's existence. This also applies to everything else you focus upon.

Let us say that one of your biggest worries in life right now is lack of financial funds. This is one area that applies to a large percentage of us. If you constantly think from day to day that you are lacking money, you are also energizing this idea from day to day. The more you focus on this lack, the more the money continues to become sparse in your life because you are energizing the idea that you have no money, and this is the message you are sending out to the universe. Using your imagination, visualization process, and positive thinking, you can change this lacking into abundance. Insteadof focusing on the problem, our angels want us to focus on the solution we would like, thus, energizing the solution energy instead of the lacking energy. If our minds are going to always energize our thoughts, the idea of having negative and worrisome thoughts becomes less logical.

The angels mention that once we create this thought or idea, depending on our reaction to it, positive or negative, we create an outcome or manifestation. An individual who constantly sees fear in their life will deal with more misery and complications than the average person. Another person who sees hope and possibilities will experience more achievements. We have no limitations when it comes to imagination and visualization and it was designed to be exactly that way! Famous thinkers, inventors, writers, and artists began their great work by first mentally inventing the possibility of such ideas becoming real. God did not create us to be limited in any fashion or form, we however, are great at creating these limitations. I have met many individuals who have told me that they have been through some very rough times in their lives yet, when they really needed some help, they pray to God, and God finds a way to give them something they prayed for. Not to take away from God's ability to grant us things in life, but these people are also using their minds to focus on a need, which eventually becomes their reality in union with God's blessing.

Let us take a look at the lack of financial gains, an area of much worry in many of the clients who come to see me, and is usually a concern for most of us as well. If at night, right before we go to sleep, we can follow this simple exercise, it will create more financial opportunities for you. Visualize yourself going to the bank every day making one deposit after another. Your mind has a very difficult time distinguishing between your imagination and reality.

By seeing yourself making these deposits in your mind over and over, the mind starts accepting this as a process of your everyday life. It energizes these thoughts and begins to release them out into the universe. The universe, in order to turn these thoughts into reality, will need to create opportunities in your life, which will bring financial gain and place you in a position of making more deposits into your bank account. Realize this does not mean that you become a millionaire overnight. What it does mean, is that opportunities and changes will arise in your life, which if you accept, will lead you into increasing your flow of financial gain. You can also visualize yourself coming home, opening the mail, and finding a check for five thousand dollars in your name. The angels do not care what image you use, just do not create limitations, and always create this image for your best and highest good with no detriment to others. You are now manifesting possibilities to eliminate your financial problems, rather than focusing on the lack, that will simply bring more of the same.

Another example of the focusing technique comes from an experience in my own personal life. This one involves using visualization to avoid a dangerous health issue. At the age of nineteen I was attending college on a partial scholarship for academics. I was very active in sports, and was starting to work for the local telephone company. I began having a dull pain in my lower back that simply would not go away. I eventually sought the help of a physician who decided to run some tests and x-rays. Finally, it was concluded that I had a small tumor surrounding my lower spine. Due to the location of the tumor and it's size, the doctors informed me that any type of surgery could lead to a possible partial or total paralysis, because the tumor was connected directly to the spine. This was back in the seventies when many of the modern medical technology used today, was not available. I asked the doctor to give me some time to decide on the course of treatment I wanted to purse. He was hesitant because as time went by the tumor would continue to grow and create further complications. A partial biopsy performed also showed abnormal cell growth which could have led to cancer as well. Eventually, he agreed to give me a week to make a decision. My choices consisted of having surgery and being paralyzed in one form or another, ignoring the pain and possibly dealing with cancer, or use the power of my mind which was already developing psychically. At this age I had not yet developed the ability to communicate with my Guardian angel and get advice. I decided to focus on removing the problem rather than worrying about it. I couldn't see myself in a wheelchair or dealing with cancer. I was also too young to give in to the idea that my life would be cut short due to this problem. At that time, I really didn't know what meditation was however, I did know and respect that the mind was very powerful. From the many psychic and spiritual experiences I had by that age, and the fact that I had been able to heal others in my family, I knew that the situation was not hopeless. What I did was dedicate an hour to two hours every night before going to sleep and use my visualization techniques. I focused on the opposite of what the doctors were saying. They said the tumor would continue to grow, I focused on the tumor shrinking. I imagined tying a rope around the tumor, squeezing it tighter and tighter, forcing it to become smaller. Another visualization I used was imagining I had soldiers running inside my body, with machine guns blasting the tumor away. I also imagined a small hammer entering my body and smashing the tumor into small pieces. Within three to four days, a great deal of the pain began to disappear. I continued the visualization techniques for another six days, longer than the doctor wanted me to wait, then I returned to the hospital for a follow up test. The new x-rays and tests showed the entire tumor had disappeared with no trace of abnormal cell growth being found in that area of the spine!

    I have used this technique in my life numerous times, not only for health issues, but to bring about changes in my career. While working construction for the phone company, a serious accident forced me to walk away from outdoor work, and enter into a desk job within the company. I was transferred to an office where I had to learn to use computers and work over the phone with customers. The idea of going from an independent outside work environment, with a list of jobs for the day that I could handle according to my daily schedule, to an indoor stuffy office with no sense of freedom was simply horrible. I decided it was time for a change. Most of the co-workers in this department had a great deal more seniority than

I did, so I knew the idea of possibly being promoted or transferred somewhere better was hopeless. Since I worked on a computer daily with a password to sign on, I decided to put the power of the mind to a test once again. I changed my password to "projun94", this was January of 1994. I had roughly sixteen years with the company, and was stressed and needed a change. The "pro" part of my new password stood for promotion, while the "jun94" part, stood for the time I allotted for this promotion to become a reality. I would see this password every single day and focused on the meaning behind it. Call it destiny or life mission, my Guardian angel and life played out their roles, and a month later, my supervisor who apparently saw potential in me, asked if I would take a test for upper management. I passed the test, and in May of 1994 was approved for a new position as Manager effective June of 1994!

We need to learn to focus on those things that will enhance our lives, rather than recycle those issues which have brought hardships to our existence. We might not be able to turn our lives around overnight simply by seeing the outcomes we want but, we will definitely create the changes which will bring about those outcomes much faster. We can speed up the process of removing or relieving unwanted situations in our lives much faster, instead of focusing and worrying about those issues which block our paths. Knowing that we do have a say in how our lives play out, can assist us in seeing obstacles as temporary roadblocks or lessons, and not simply as dead ends. We need to know that we have the capability of bringing about those experiences which will enhance our ability to accomplish our life missions. By focusing on our ability to overcome issues, we not only avoid further complications but, have a better chance of raising the bar from fifty to sixty percent life mission completion upon our deaths. Our angels want us to take responsibility of our lives and not wait until someone or something else comes along. Destiny will play it's part, but all of us need to focus on what our hearts, minds, and souls wish to accomplish.

AFFIRMATIONS TO USE IN AREAS OF FOCUS:

An affirmation is simply a written phrase that you can read daily to assist you in accomplishing a goal, or removing an obstacle. Below are six general affirmations we can all use in our daily lives. You can also add or create your own depending on the situation at hand which you wish to improve. Remember, once again, these affirmations should be written for your best and highest good, with no negative outcomes to others. These can be placed in areas where you are forced to see them daily such as, on the bathroom mirror, refrigerator, or by your night stand.

Note: make these affirmations as detailed as you can or as simple as you like.

1. I have the clarity to change and bring about solutions in all obstacles placed before me.

2. I realize that all that happens in my path is for best and highest good.

3. As a co-creator in this universe I can bring about the changes I need in my life.

4. There are no hidden agendas in my life's path, just hidden surprises to enhance my life.

5. I can see solutions to setbacks which enter my life.

6. The more I focus on positive possibilities, the more riches and strengths I discover about myself.

Chapter 7

Fifth Message: Letting Go

An important area of our lives that our Guardian angels feel we need to improve is the ability to release and let go of difficult issues from our past. First, need to make an effort to understand them, make the necessary changes they bring about, and walk away from them and not continue to rewind them over and over in our minds. This message area deserves it's own chapter, even though the idea has been discussed in union with some of the prior messages. This problem applies to so many different areas of our lives, and when it is not under control can be extremely destructive. When we speak of letting go in this chapter, we are referring strictly to negative and difficult experiences. When we recall positive incidents in our lives, they actually produce positive vibrations, which in turn enhances our abilities to move forward. So all those fond memories you have of your life thus far, feel free to reminisce them as frequently as you would like, with no limitations.

All of us, at one time or another, will experience a hardship in our lives, which we will consider to be unjust or undeserving. These are all part of teaching us to adjust, mature, and discover our inner strengths. These cover everything from love relationships that have ended, deaths of loved ones, divorces, illnesses, and financial or natural disasters, just to name a few. No one really plans or prepares themselves to go through these type of events, which force us to deal with them in a shocking abrupt manner. We do not wake up every morning wondering if today is the day that the house accidently burns down, or if your love mate will decide not to come home again. We program ourselves to handle the daily routine of our existence. Even though we do not plan for these types of experiences, they still occur every day. Eventually, unless you entered a lifetime of pure bliss, you will be hit with a hardship, and the trauma will settle in.

As humans, we constantly look forward to positive events in our lives, almost as just rewards for the challenges we have to endure. When confronted with an unexpected negative event, we are usually caught off guard. As children, we are usually taught that you will be rewarded for good behavior. This concept is engraved in our minds as our parents find ways of getting us to help out around the house, then followed in school, where grades are given upon our best results. During the first few years of school, we are thrown into competition and acceptance. Children are also told to get the best grades in school or to become the best athlete, as these actions in the long run, bring about the best rewards as scholarships, popularity, respect from our peers and teachers alike. By the time we are in junior high school, we have been conditioned to think that in order to achieve in life, we must struggle to do better than those around us. As we grow into adults, we use this same philosophy, that as long as we are good and work hard, we will be rewarded in life. The sad thing is that this is not always true. Most of us, as adults, continue to find ourselves continuously in some level of struggle where the rewards do not balance the hardships.

Society tells us that the better we are and the more we achieve, the better chances we have in the so-called real world. Many of us depend on this need to constantly achieve in order to elevate our self esteem. As we enter college and adulthood, this turns into a constant struggle or effort to find the perfect mate, job, home, car, and social status. It is not until we get much older, that we realize we have spent so much time looking for recognition, that we have failed to give it to those around us whom we love. Due to this emphasis on achievement, especially in the United States, so many people are in various levels of depression, extremely stressed out in their employment, and are dealing with negative aspects of low self esteem and lack of accomplishment.

Taking all the above mentioned issues into consideration, we live from day to day waiting for the next opening or opportunity which will take us higher on the ladder of success. If one day the next step happens to be a negative situation, we are destroyed emotionally and psychologically, because the expected reward turns out to be a punishment. Our Guardian angels say that we connect so quickly with anger and hatred when we have a setback, that we actually create an emotional blockage of energy. This blockage is continuously fed every time we think about it over and over. As I have mentioned many times before, thoughts have energy and intent, and whenever we take the time to rewind that thought and give it more emphasis, we also add to this initial blockage. This blockage will continue to receive energy until it can no longer hold the overflow. Like the laws of physics tell us, when an overflow is created, it eventually needs to be released. When our emotional blockages explode it will be displayed as a mental or physical setback.

No memory is ever lost. We are responsible for storing all our memories in our cellular bodies from all our lifetimes. What we teach ourselves to do is to eventually block out the difficult ones from our conscious minds. They are blocked out from our ability to consciously deal with them however, they are still packed with energy in our mind, body, and soul. This charged memory still exists at a very potent level in our subconscious mind, and will eventually need to be dealt with. This is why I strongly believe in individuals having regressions done to resolve unexplained challenges in their current lives. On many occasions, a past life memory or past life incident that was blocked, will manifest as some form of challenge in the next life.

Letting go, releasing, and understanding the challenges we encounter in our lives are essential in allowing us to maintain a healthy lifestyle. Letting go goes hand in hand with the previous message involving focus. It's actually the step which is required right before focus. When we are placed in a difficult or negative situation, we first need to experience it, release it, and then focus on the best way to handle it. If we are unable to let it go, the energy behind the process of focusing becomes very weak, and eventually has no means of positive productivity.

Forgiveness is another strong element involved in the process of letting go. It's an extremely powerful process in which we are allowed to continue in our journey. Before I indulge further into the process of forgiveness, allow me to share a case I had which will illustrate the point I am trying to make. A woman in her late forties came to see me for a reading mainly for health problems and inability to become pregnant. During her reading, her angel informed us that many of her issues were originating from a situation in her most recent past life.

Whenever a Guardian angel decides to inform me of someone's past life, an energetic screen opens in mid-air behind the person, maybe five feet wide by three feet high. It reminds me of the old projector movies that my father used to show me as a child. I get to see the events of the individual's life as well as hear the conversations that took place. It is one of my psychic abilities which I have done thousands of times, yet I am still baffled when it occurs.

In this woman's past life she was female, the oldest child among six, living in Western Europe during the early 1800's. At a young age, due to economic difficulties in her family, she was removed from school by her parents to help out around the house and take care of her sisters and brothers. By the time she was fifteen she resembled a mother of thirty. She longed to escape this lifestyle, and decided at seventeen years old to wed a man she didn't love as a way of escaping from all the responsibilities in her home. In addition to all the chores she had to do, she also had a challenging relationship with both her parents and had no level of communication with them. She felt trapped and unappreciated, and the idea of only worrying about one person, instead of an entire household, couldn't be much worse. The man she married was ten years older, a hard worker, and a bit more settled financially than her parents had been. He truly adored her, but in her heart she could not reciprocate the same feelings towards him. She had basically used this marriage as a form of independence from her family. She even tried to avoid sexual contact with her husband in fear that if she became pregnant, she would be forced to have additional ties to him. Her goal was to stay with him for a year or so, save some money, and find a way to leave him and gain the freedom to do whatever she wanted. After a few months of marriage, she could no longer avoid his persistence and was forced on occasion to entertain him sexually. She was afraid he would abandon her before she could put her plan in action. Eight months into the marriage she discovers she was pregnant! She was afraid that disclosing this information to him would complicate her plans, so she needed to come up with a resolution to this situation quickly. Not being school trained, she lacked tactfulness in communication, did not know how to read properly, and had no knowledge of exactly how this pregnancy would develop. She had seen her mother pregnant many times and knew the hardships involved especially in the last few months. She also lacked a certain level of reasoning and common sense and was becoming anxious as the days passed. One night she found herself alone at home and in desperation, began to drink alcohol to calm her nerves. After a few hours and becoming intoxicated she came up with a wild idea. She stripped off her clothes, walked over to the fireplace, and grabbed an iron rod. She placed the tip of the rod in the fire and held it there for a few minutes until it was glowing from the heat. She took a deep breath, laid down on the floor, spread her legs and inserted the rod into herself as deep as she could. She let out a horrible scream as the pain of the hot rod entering her flesh was unbearable. She quickly fainted from the excruciating pain and the sight of blood flowing everywhere.

    Her husband arrive shortly after to find his wife on the floor, naked, motionless, and covered in blood from the waist down. He lifted her and realized she was breathing. He covered her and rode his carriage as quickly as he could to the nearest doctor. The doctor was able to stop the bleeding and save her life. When she eventually recovered, she was told that not only had she killed her unborn child, but she also destroyed any chances of having other children in the future. Upon realizing that she had done this intentionally, her husband in rage threw her out of the house, and she was looked upon as an outcast by the entire community. No other man, even though she was attractive, would give her the time of day. She began to sink more and more into depression as the years went by. She refused to go back to her family and lived alone in a boarding house where she eventually took up prostitution as a way of surviving.

One night in her late thirties, after fruitless attempts to gain some type of emotional balance in her life, she decided that maybe suicide was the only answer. Deep inside she knew that she lacked the courage to take her life, so she decided to just go for a walk. She walked out through the rear of her dwelling and wandered for hours aimlessly in the darkness. All she could see was the outline of tall trees and the shadowy figures made around her by the glow of the full moon. She dropped to her knees and began to cry. Filled with anger and rage, she looked up at the sky, and began to yell at God for ruining her life. She told God that she hated him, that she didn't need anyone in her life, she didn't need children or parents who cared for her, that she could survive on her own. After some time she picked herself up from the ground and slowly went back to her home. She ended up dying three years later due to complications in her heart.

According to our angels, when we reach the moment of death, we get an opportunity to review our lives. We see a video of all our accomplishments, failures, and faults. In her review, this woman's spirit could not let go of the anger she had accumulated throughout the life she had just lost. She was upset that nothing in her life ever turned out right, especially her inability to find true love and have children. Her spirit's failure to let go of these issues and her decision to come back into her present life was now forcing her to deal with the consequences. The difficult situations in her present life were a direct cause of what she was not able to release in her past life. Now, she was not able to hold onto a relationship for more than two years. She said her partners would treat her like trash and abuse her. She was not able to have a child even though medically there was no reason for it. To make matters worse, her mother in this life abandoned her at the age of seventeen, when she was killed in an alley during the act of prostitution.

Her angel explained that when we, in a moment of pure rage, make a statement derived from anger and hatred, this statement becomes engraved in the memory of our soul. If we are not able to release it and let it go properly in the spirit state, it will eventually play out as an unresolved issue in our current life. This shows us two lessons which are very crucial. It shows us just how powerful our soul and mind can be, as well as how delicate they can be when charged with negative energy. This client abandoned her family in her past life when she was seventeen, and in this life her mother was taken away from her at the same age. She destroyed her child in her past life to avoid the responsibility of bearing a child with a man she did not love. In this life, she could not bear children and could not find any man that would love her. She turned to prostitution in her past life due to desperation and lack of education or skills. In this life, her mother lost her life due to prostitution. This woman also shared with me that she did not finish college because of fear of not graduating and experiencing more failure. Subconsciously, by holding on to everything that went wrong in her past life, she had created avenues of failures and disappointments in her current voyage. The beautiful aspect of regressions, whether done under hypnosis or though a psychic channel as myself, is that when the individual truly understands the cause for many of their problems, they have a much better chance to release them and change for the better.

With the above example, we are shown the perils of holding on to negative issues, as an eternal downfall. Doing this can harm us in the development of our current lifetime as well as, the possibility of a future one. This is why I always tell my audience, whenever I have a speaking engagement, to let go of difficult experiences. Try and deal with unresolved issues in a positive way, do not hold grudges, and always seek ways to release unwanted angers. Divorces, deaths, financial and emotional failures, need to be understood and processed. They will to a degree allow us to grow as humans and express ourselves as spiritual beings. They are not meant to stunt our growth or stop us in our tracks. These experiences are sometimes requested by us before we are born to assist us in learning specific lessons. Our angels inform us that we have a great deal of control over many of our experiences, and the way we choose to handle them will determine how we move forward in our lives.

This brings us back to the element of forgiveness. Forgiveness is not an easy thing to do, but it can serve as an incredible tool to assist us in balancing our lives. The ability to forgive creates an energy flow which goes in direct contrast to negative vibrations. This tool can be expressed to another individual who has caused you pain or even to a situation God placed in your path which created hardship in your life. You can also forgive yourself for an action or act you were responsible for. All of us need to call time out and review our lives at different points. We need to see if we are holding on to any resentments or negative experiences. We need to seriously release and let them go in order to avoid an imbalance of energy which can destroy us emotionally, mentally, physically, or spiritually.

I want you to understand that when I say we need to let go of negative things in life, this does not mean that you simply go about accepting challenges without anger or resentment. Those emotions are part of being human. What I want to focus on is to discover a way of dealing with it after the anger and resentment have settled in. Once you get upset, you need to focus on creating a change or taking an action, which will compensate for the negative issue at hand. Find a solution for the unexpected turn of events, and then let go of the original anger. Again, this is not an easy thing to do, and in my readings almost eighty percent of the time, these issues are floating in the person's life. I have seen so many clients that come to me with old anger patterns which have prevented them from being fully functional loving human beings. In these cases I have to be both the psychic and counselor to mediate between my client, their Guardian angel, and the information that has to be resolved and released. I have to assist the client in understanding the cause of the anger, and suggest ways to change so that upcoming events in their lives will be understood and used to help them move forward in a positive manner.

Exercise Used in the Process of Letting Go:

There is a wonderful ritual which my old business partner and I performed in many of our classes which we used to aid in the process of letting go and forgiving. It is known as the Burning Bowl Ceremony. It's used by many different cultures in many ways as a means of release. You start by placing yourself in a relaxed position and enter a light state of meditation for approximately five to ten minutes. This meditation should be designed to assist you in releasing stress, to clear your mind, and connect with your higher self. Your higher self simply is that part of your mind and soul that accepts the total being you are, and is in direct connection with your highest potential. This can be accomplished by taking a few deep breaths, holding them for a count of five, release them for a count of three, and breathe in again for a count of five. Repeat this pattern until you are focusing on your breathing and not your wandering thoughts. When you have done this for five or ten minutes, slowly open your eyes and hold on to this level of relaxation.

After this short meditation, take some paper and write down everything in your life that has bothered you, bought you pain, or anything else you felt was unjust and hurtful. For some, this might take several pages, while some of you might just want to deal with just one specific issue. Really go out of your way to search through all your emotional archives and pull out all the negative setbacks you have been holding deep in your heart. After writing these words, gather your paper or papers, place them in a metal bowl which has been filled with sand or dirt. Take a match, hold the papers in your hand, burn one of the edges and drop the papers into the bowl. Continue staring into the bowl as the papers all turn into ash.

You can make this ritual very simple or you can make it very elaborate by burning candles, incense, and playing music in the background. You can use magician's paper, which when lit completely disappears into thin air, and gives you a stronger feeling that what you wrote has also disappeared from your energy. You can make a statement during the process of burning the papers to incorporate your decision of refusing to carry these burdens any further. This ritual allows you and your energy to be given permission by your higher self, to release these memories and negative vibrations from your soul, karma, your present, past, and future. This ceremony will also allow you to have more room for positive experiences to enter. Remember, what you store inside your heart creates energy, and this energy needs to be consumed with positive not negative experiences.

Below is a statement you can use to assist you during this ceremony if you cannot find words of your own. After you have written your statements, fold the papers, hold them against your heart. Repeat the following words to yourself or out loud.

"Today, I give myself permission to free my heart, soul, body, and mind from situations in my life which have hurt me, brought me sadness, or forced me to disconnect from love. I no longer wish to carry these burdens in my energy field and as of today I decide to release them back to the universe where they will be properly disposed. I now open to new positive changes, experiences, and love. I love myself too much to be burdened by old memories which no longer serve a purpose in my life. And so it is...."

Next, proceed to burn the papers, and drop them into the bowl.

This same exercise can also be done with a bit of a twist in situations where you need to ask forgiveness of someone you hurt, but are unable to do it in person either because of complications, fear, or the person is no longer living. Write a letter to this person, follow the same steps of the ceremony, and burn the letter into the bowl.

As a final word in the area of letting go, our angels want us to realize we are here in this planet to gain experiences, not necessarily to store them. Realize, no matter how old the situation may be, your mental intention to release it is what allows the energy to be removed from your existence. Sometimes, it is a good idea to repeat the Burning Bowl ceremony at various points in your life as a form of maintenance.

Chapter 8

Sixth Message: Expressing

Another area of our lives which our Guardian angels feel we have a struggle with is our inability to verbally express our feelings. They tell me that we have such a hard time expressing positive statements yet, even as a child, we have no hesitation expressing negative or harmful comments. It is so natural and easy for us, when angry or upset, to say something hurtful or derogatory. On the other hand, it is quite a challenge to look someone in the eye and share a positive or strengthening remark. The worst part of this weakness is that many times we wait so long to make that positive statement, that we totally lose the opportunity, and are left regretting it later in our lives. I am referring to simple statements like "Thanks" or "I love you", which we rationalize a million times before the words come out of our mouth. Either embarrassment or awkwardness gets in the way, we put the statement on hold, and then realize we have lost the chance to express it. Sometimes we lose contact with that person because they are no longer living, or we feel that too much time has passed and it is better off left alone.

Many people go see psychics and mediums because they wish to connect with someone they knew that is no longer in the physical plane. They feel there is some unfinished business left behind and now when the person is no longer alive, they want to have another opportunity to clear the air. Sadly, many of these unfinished businesses, have to do with never saying thanks or never showing gratitude for something in the past. I can truly relate to this chapter's message because I was raised in a family atmosphere where verbal communication was very limited during my first fourteen years. My parents, my sister, and myself all loved each other, but never went out of our way to express it verbally. My parents in general were very shy, and I was raised thinking that speaking freely was not normal. The idea of kissing or hugging someone close to you was unheard of. Outside of an occasional hug or kiss goodnight before bedtime by my mother, I witnessed limited contact verbally or physically, by my family. We rarely expressed physical or verbal recognition of love, but we had no difficulty screaming or yelling when we were upset. The awkward thing was that even though it was not shown frequently to us, my parents expected me and my sister to express affection, easily to others. One example of this was when I was a child, and I have to visit my great grandmother, who I only saw once or twice a year. I used to have a fear of very old people and my great grandmother was in her late eighties. My parents would give me that look to go over and give her a hug as soon as we walked into her house. She would then proceed to suffocate me inside her chest and it seemed like forever before I was released. It was very uncomfortable to be so physically close to someone who I just felt was a stranger, even though she did everything to make me and my sister feel welcomed and loved. I didn't understand the importance of showing this physical affection when it was not a requirement around our home.

It was not until after my graduation from high school that I noticed my mother opening more socially with strangers and showing a much stronger affectionate side to my sister and me. We had moved from New York to Miami, Florida and maybe the laid back atmosphere that Miami had in the 70's allowed my family to open up more. Being raised in this no touchy, no hugging, no kissing atmosphere as a child, made it difficult for me to open up and share some of the difficult psychic experiences I was encountering. I was extremely shy, partly because of my parent's shyness and, partly because of the fact I led a double life with my psychic lifestyle hidden from my friends and overall family members. I hid this psychic part of myself to avoid ridicule, rejection, and I figured that if I didn't discuss it with anyone, it would go away.

Right after high school is when I began to open up more socially. I got involved in college activities and became more outspoken regarding my ideas and beliefs. By this time I was aware of my healing abilities and every now and than, would assist some friend or acquaintance of the family who was dealing with a health issue. Many times they wanted to give me a big hug for the assistance I had given them and this was very awkward for me. The idea of a total stranger hugging me just didn't fit well with my idea of social behavior. I would quickly but politely walk away from the hug, and start a conversation to get the person involved in something else. Even up to my early thirties, I still was trying to dust the shyness which would occasionally fall on my personality. I remember one time I decided to visit the Unity Church in my desperate search for some type of religious structure. Unknown to me, one of their rituals which occurred ten minutes into the service, was to turn around and hug the person next to you. I just wanted to make a mad dash to the exit doors and keep on running. There was not just one, but several people, anxiously waiting their turn to hug me! Even though I enjoyed the opening meditation, I managed to arrive late to the following services to skip the hugging part. After some time, I began to see the sincerity and love among these strangers who just wanted to give me an embrace, as a sign of love. Eventually I was there bright and early eagerly looking for my next hugging victim!

Over the years, I have finally understood the value of positive physical and verbal expression. Working with clients from all parts of the world I can appreciate the universal need to be appreciated by others. The sad truth is that more than fifty percent of individuals still fear the idea of being hugged or, receiving a verbal compliment. So, not only is it difficult for some to express it but, also to receive it, as it was for me in my early years. To this day, I have yet to master the art of hugging but, have made some huge strides compared to my younger days.

The Guardian angels say that we are all teachers, healers, and guardians for each other. Understanding this, we are still afraid to express love, sympathy, or simply trust our hearts, and share some advice or wisdom because of fear of rejection. Rejection can be so devastating that we choose to avoid it as much as possible. Avoiding a situation that will possibly open the door to rejection, is the easiest way for us to cope with confrontations. Many times we gather all those positive feelings for others and think that one day when all is perfect, and we are able to handle any rejections, we will release a truckload of positive verbal and physical expressions on someone's doorstep. Once again, life can get complicated, and those few precious moments we have to share cannot be ignored or saved for a more appropriate time.

As humans, we actually have more in common than we might imagine. Our angels say that if we realize just how much we resemble each other, maybe we can realize that by working together, many issues and differences can be resolved. If we can work in harmony, express ideas and feelings, and form a common goal, we would lose a lot of the fears and inhibitions which make it difficult for us to co-exist on this planet. Realizing how good we feel when we get a positive statement told to us, should be an incentive to give that same feeling back to someone else. Remember, a positive expression can be verbal, physical, or shown with a simple gesture of appreciation. Out of all of these forms, verbal continues to be the most difficult to be expressed.

One day a young man of eighteen or nineteen came to my office for a reading. He was quite nervous from the moment he stepped in. I do realize most of my clients enter a bit cautiously because, they know they are about to meet their Guardian angel and get information about their life and, that can be a bit intimidating. In this young man's case, the nervousness was a bit more than usual. From the moment he sat down he could not stay still in his chair. I tried to settle him down by explaining the process of the reading, and adding some humor about spirituality. I could see all he wanted was to get the reading over with and get out of my office as fast as possible. As I was about to start the session, he asked if he could ask a question to his angel, to receive some guidance in a particular area of his life. I told him of course he could ask as many questions as he wanted to but, he quickly said no, it was just one particular one that he was worried about.

Looking down at the floor he barely whispered the question to me. His voice was so low I could not understand him and asked him to please repeat it again. Without looking up, he repeated the question a bit louder, and asked me to make sure I passed it on to his angel. His question revolved around the idea of wanting to know if his parents loved him. Upon hearing the question, I assumed maybe he was adopted, maybe he lost his parents at a young age, or maybe he was forced to live away from his parents at an early age and, never had a chance to know this. It turned out, he still was living at home with his parents, the youngest of seven children, and everything was always so hectic at home that he barely spoke to his parents. He did not want to interfere with their busy lifestyles and realistically, never had any quality time to sit around and chat with them. This poor young man had spent eighteen years with both parents and had never been told that he was loved. He was never shown or rewarded with love in a suitable fashion that would have given clarity to his question. Remembering my early years, I could relate to the verbal lack of love from my parents as a child, but his case seemed more severe. Even though my parents did not constantly embrace me with hugs, they provided me with support and love by sacrificing so much to help me understand and deal with my psychic challenges. Anyone would have thought that a man of eighteen, living with his parents, would have been constantly in the atmosphere of parental love. Unfortunately this was not the case for my client and many other children in this world. He was pleased when told that his parents did truly love him but had a difficult time expressing it. His angel also gave him examples of things they had done for him throughout the years to show the love they had for him. He was told how their way of expressing love to him was limited due to all the other children's needs but he was constantly in their hearts and in their decision making process. This information was so extremely valuable to this young man's ability to feel love.

Another negative aspect of the inability to express love verbally for those we care about, is the fact that this blockage, just like the previous chapter, can carry over with us into the spirit state. So many people have died without the chance to say something to someone that was so valuable to them. Many times, this lost opportunity does not allow the spirit to rest in peace, and forces them not to accept their death until they can accomplish this feat. I have worked with many spirits who are struggling in their realm because, they cannot let go of their physical anchor to the material world due to some level of closure that was left unattended. This unsettled closure can sometimes lead to a haunting, not because the spirit wishes to do harm, but because they cannot rest until certain things are resolved. The non-tranquil state of the spirit can last from a few days to eternity. This is where the work of certain psychics and mediums who can speak with the dead, becomes so essential and rewarding. The ability to give an individual one more chance to say something to someone who has crossed over, or visa versa , can be so powerful. It permits both the spirit and the individual a chance to have closure and continue on their transition. This shows us the importance of opening and expressing our feelings, especially when it is to share love, gratitude, or simple appreciation.

There is yet another negative aspect of holding back, or not expressing our feelings and emotions. Our angels say we must understand the theory that everything is energy. When we hold these unshared or trapped emotions inside for a long period of time, they turn into destructive energy. After so many years, as we mentioned in the chapter on health, this energy will create an imbalance in the physical body. I had another case in which a 45 year old woman was so distraught over the death of her father. The fact that she never took the time to thank him for all he did for her throughout her life really destroyed her. The more she thought about the idea of not speaking out and sharing when she had the chance the more she noticed a soreness in her throat area. It became so bad that she eventually developed a physical challenge swallowing food. Doctors and physical therapists worked with her with no success. Upon understanding the correlation between her anguish and her throat area, she was able to release the physical problem shortly thereafter. Never lose the opportunity to express and say what your heart truly wishes to express. It is essential for your growth, your spirit, and at times, even your health.

Meditation to assist us in our ability to Express:

Follow the steps discussed earlier to reach a relaxed state of mind and body. Open your imagination, and create a place where all the people you have been waiting to say something to are gathered. Imagine them all sitting in individual booths. Depending on how many people you are working with, obviously will determine the number of booths you have around you. Each booth is enclosed in sound proof glass as well as a surrounding curtain. You will share whatever you need to share with each person three different ways.

One at a time, you approach each booth, and pick up a pencil and pad already provided.

The curtain is drawn around the booth so they cannot see you. You first write what you wish to tell them than drop it through a slot on the top of the booth so the person inside can read your words. You go around to all the booths following the same procedure.

The second time, you go back to each booth, press the button that says audio, allowing them to hear the same words you wrote to them but, this time coming from your voice. While doing this to each booth, try to imagine what their faces look like, as they hear you finally saying the words you have been keeping inside for so long. After finishing with all the booths, you now have a more comfortable feeling knowing they have read and heard all your words. Next, approach each booth, release the curtain and open the door. Allow each person to stand in front of you and once again, repeat the words to them face to face. Hold their hand and look them in the eye as you repeat your words for the final time. Realize this exercise is for your heart and soul. How they handle or respond to your message is not as important as your ability to share it with them. Feel the joy of being able to express your emotions and feelings with no sense of rejection, but rather, total acceptance. Before you walk away from each person, give them the chance to maybe give you some feedback or share some words with you as well.

This meditative exercise will allow you, from an energetic approach, to release the stress and negativity of holding on to expressions of communication which have been locked inside and never released. The entire exercise should not take more than fifteen to twenty minutes, yet the end results are positively endless.

Chapter 9

Seventh Message: Mergence

This next area of messages from our Guardian angels is one of extreme importance to humanity as a whole. According to our heavenly helpers, a shift of energy is taking place between the Spirit Realm and the Earth plane, a shift that is affecting everyone on this planet. There is an energetic attraction between these two worlds which can be best described as a mergence. In order to understand this process, we need to be aware of a situation that has been taking place on our planet over the last twenty years. Throughout recorded time mankind has been a witness to many spiritual wonders such as miracles, visions, angelic encounters, and at times, extraterrestrial encounters. Over the last two decades, these experiences have been reported at a much higher frequency.

In addition to the higher amount of reported cases, these experiences are also being reported throughout a larger area of the planet. Regardless of what area of the world these encounters are being reported, and what religious backgrounds these areas hold, these reported experiences all have the same similarities. For example, the vision of the Blessed Virgin Mary has been seen throughout the planet, even though this symbolic vision is normally associated with those of the Catholic faith.

According to our angels, we are receiving a wake up call, as well as a request from the higher levels of spiritual planes. The reason I say planes in plural is because these requests are being brought down to us from various spiritual dimensions. These dimensions co-exist to form what many of us call Heaven or the Spirit world. Included in these dimensions is the Spirit plane where we enter once we die and cross over from the physical or material existence. Other sub-dimensions exist where Spirit guides and Spiritual Teachers dwell to assist others. Even higher, we have various levels of the Angelic Realm, which oversee most of the energies represented upon our planet. The request we are getting from these dimensions is that we, as humans, need to make some changes, because we are holding a high level of negativity. The danger is that this level of negativity is now starting to cross over with us upon our deaths to the higher realms of existence.

Bottom line, we are polluting these higher realms of existence, as we make our attempts to reconnect with the God Source. It is the same idea as an individual who has a virus, ignores the danger it carries, and goes around infecting others who they come in contact with. The negativity we hold at the moment of our death does not disappear or stay behind with our physical remains. We, as humans, take our emotions, fears, and insecurities with us as we adjust to a new level of existence in the spirit world. The overall negativity on our planet has reached an all time high, and we are basically now bringing some of it into the spirit world. We are creating a new level of unbalance that has never existed before in this realm.

We are constantly receiving proof of the afterlife through visions and encounters that many individuals are having. Many of these encounters have a common thread. Many of those who have died and crossed over into spirt are at unrest over negative unresolved issues left behind. There are also many negative or evil people who are dying holding a great deal of anger and evil within their soul. These spirits are also entering the Spirit realm carrying these emotions with them with a fury. So, our Spiritual helpers, whose responsibility is to oversee the Spirit realm are seeing an energetic pollution entering their world. They are worried that as we continue to develop from one dimension to another we will also continue to taint each level with even more negativity.

The angels have told me that we are all on a ladder, where every step of the ladder represents another dimension which leads back to the God Source. Each ladder is a separate dimension in which every being in that dimension is working it's way to eventually climb out of that step and up to the next step above. Eventually all of us will reach a life, where upon our death, we make the decision not to enter back into another physical body. We will reach a level of total completion in which all lessons have been learned and we consciously close the doors to the physical world. At that point we start to climb up to the next step on the ladder or the next dimension to learn all aspects of the Spirit realm. As time evolves, we will again eventually leave that realm, and cross over to the next dimension. This is the basis of our Spiritual evolution. Every time we step up the ladder, the being of who and what we are, becomes part of that new dimension. If that beingness is not totally clear of negativity, we than become the virus that will create problems in that new realm.

Now we start to develop a better understanding as to the urgency of getting our acts together as individuals, because of how we affect other levels. Now let us look at this same idea, not through the sense of individuals, but as a whole. As mankind has evolved throughout the years, the physical planet has also made some adjustments. The energies and vibrations which make up our physical world have been fine tuned and adjusted to flow with the overall scheme of things. It has already been documented and proven by physicists that the speed of our planet rotating on it's own axis has increased. Remembering that we are all made of energy, and are affected by vibrations and frequencies, this increase in speed also affects our individual process of functioning. Look at it as though we were all magnets, and when faster or stronger magnetic pulls around us are increased, we have no choice but to follow or repel this new attraction.

The way we are individually being affected by this increase in speed, has a direct outcome in what we absorb and take into the spirit realm when we die. Let us take the reference of the ladder that we used earlier to make this clearer. We will give the ladder seven steps from top to bottom. Down on the second step, we have our physical world, while up on top is the God Source. I am only using these seven steps symbolically as a numerical example, I am not saying that there are seven dimensions in total from top to bottom. I would need an entire second book to get into that explanation. Every step of the ladder that we climb, the vibrational force of that step is much faster, and the knowledge higher. We in a human form, vibrate at a much slower speed than those in Spirit, obviously because of the density of our physical body, and those in Spirit vibrate slower than the Angelic Realm.

The same can be said of varying vibrations among one human to another. Depending on an individual's growth, maturity, understanding of love and spirituality, among other things, each individual will have a different vibratory rate. A religious figure, such as the Pope, has been known to emit a certain air or energy around them that people recognize, or feel while in their presence. A truly gifted performer, such as a piano player, gives out an energy of brilliance and artistic capability. Some people are intimidated to be around a scholar or a genius because they feel their own energy is unequal to that of that person.

On the other hand, a very negative person, down in their luck, will be totally ignored or unseen in a crowded restaurant due to their low vibrations. A very depressed or sick individual will have very low vibrations and be lacking in energy. Some of us who have evolved spiritually and psychically, can increase the vibrations around our energetic body, to tap into a higher realm, such as the world of spirits. This is what many psychics and mediums, such as myself, do in order to be able to communicate or visually see those in Spirit or in the Angelic realms. We charge up our energy in order to be more compatible with the level of source we are attempting to communicate with. It is like turning the knob on a radio until we find the perfect level or frequency where the music comes in very clearly.

For example, if I am attempting to connect with a spirit close to me, I raise my energy and mind consciousness to their level. If I am getting ready to do an Angel reading, I have to raise the energy even higher to be able to see the individual's Guardian angel and obtain information. In a few paragraphs, I have given you a concept of understanding that we exist in different levels of vibrations within our own planet, as well as other dimensions. I have also mentioned that we are unconsciously polluting the next level we enter upon our death, by holding onto a great deal of negativity. With that as a background, let us now focus on the idea of mergence, which our angels feel we truly need to understand. This is the mergence of our physical world with that of our next level, which is the Spirit realm. This mergence is taking place, because many souls are finally reaching a level of fulfillment after death, in which they are deciding not to re-enter another physical incarnation ever again. According to our Angelic helpers, a little less than seven percent of the planet's population, is attempting to work and complete their last physical incarnation.

As we evolve Spiritually and make the conscious decision not to return to the physical plane, we bring into the Spirit world a certain energetic pull. It is almost, as if we were connected by an imaginary string to the physical world, the same way a child is connected by the umbilical cord to it's mother. As more and more of us evolve to this evolutionary status the pull becomes stronger. In addition, as other less developed souls continue to bring in more negativity into the spirit plane, they create a density which in turn, slows down the vibration of that plane. So as we can see, in one aspect we are pulling in energy from the physical world, and on the other scale, we are slowing the vibrations of the Spirit world. As the vibration of Spirit world decreases, it becomes more attainable to us in the physical world. This leads us into the idea that a mergence is taking place between these two worlds.

As humans discover how to raise their energies to coincide closer with that of the next highest realm, we will be able to have a broader level of communication and accessibility to the spirit state. In the future, speaking to loved ones who have died, having insights to future possibilities, and gaining more clarity of our life missions, are all avenues which will be more accessible to us. As I mentioned before, with the speed of our physical planet increasing, we as humans are also being pushed to maintain pace with this new level of equilibrium. How has this added speed affected us so far?

In the last ten years mankind has struggled more than ever to gain a sense of grounding or foundation. Many years ago when I first started doing readings, the top two questions were related to love life and finances. In the last few years these two questions have been replaced by individuals wanting to know their purpose in this life.

Many individuals are feeling lost, disconnected to their religion or faith, unsure of their roles with family, friends, and work conditions. Many have a stronger desire to find peace, tranquility, and love within themselves, even if it means disconnecting from others. They are slowly losing their desire to climb the social ladder of success and financial power. There has been a strong surge of depression in our society because of this sense of being lost, disconnected, or having no direction in their lives. Many high powered executives are leaving behind their hectic lifestyles, and trading them for a chance to exist in a quiet country setting, where they can relate and work on their own development. Many individuals now wish to dedicate more energy to saving the planet instead of saving or increasing the value of their company. The scary thing is, that this new faster vibration upon our planet is a one way process. It will maintain levels of stability which are presently existing or continue increasing, but will not go back to what it used to be. Those who refuse to accept these levels of vibrations will find themselves struggling for survival, and eventually will look for ways to shorten their life spans. This will happen because they cannot handle this new level of energy emotionally, mentally, spiritually, or even physically.

The next information I will offer is not designed to contradict or belittle any religious background or dogma. We need to understand the overall game plan behind all living energy and conscious existence. Before mankind was created, the Source's or God's plan was to break apart from an all knowing and all loving matter, and downgrade to various levels or dimensions. Each level would have specific responsibilities, and eventually work it's way down to physical living matter, including man, dinosaurs, and living micro organisms. The angels give us the following example to assist us in understanding this process. Imagine a giant ball of yarn that was existing as a finished product but was never actually created.

In other words, this ball of yarn never had a starting point, it just existed, wrapped nice and tight in perfection. In order to truly understand itself, the Source, or this ball of yarn, decided to unravel itself to discover it's original starting point. Upon reaching that point, it would gather itself and return with the knowledge of where it originated. Our angels also tell us that humankind is at the end of this yarn, and we are now at a level in our evolution where we are being called back to our creator. Along this journey, we will pass and reconnect with all the other levels or dimensions ahead of us as we work our way back to oneness. Another way of understanding this concept is by imagining that tomorrow you wake up, are able to sit and play the piano at the same level of a professional, even though you have never played or touched a piano key in your life. You would have this incredible knowledge and ability, yet you would have no concept of how you gained this ability. The God Source had all the knowledge, love, wisdom, and intelligence, but lacked the experiences of how these levels were attained. I had an incredible regression done when I was in my early twenties which allowed me to experience this concept and I hope to share this in a book form in the future.

Now we have three basic outlines so far which all play out together. One, we have the planet increasing speed and forcing us to adapt to a new level of existence. Two, we have the spirit plane losing some of it's speed due to the negativity which we continue to bring into it. Finally, we have the concept that as a whole, humankind is starting to realize that it no longer needs to repeat more physical lives, and is evolving into pure spirit form. All of these three actions taking place, defines the concept of the mergence which our angels wish for us to understand. It is an exciting and incredible process which is being viewed and examined by all the dimensions above us. Eventually, these higher dimensions will also have to go through the same transformation, as this ball of yarn begins to wind itself back into the original ball.

In order for us to begin our journey back, we need to become more adaptable to the next level of consciousness which happens to be spirit. Having this concept in the background, the logical format for us to use to enter into this next level of existence, requires that we become more sensitive to this next level of consciousness. Theoretically speaking, our present level of existence is but a few strands of yarn. To enter the next level we must grow, expand, and cover more space. Energetically, the only way for us to expand to this next level, is to increase our awareness in order to avoid getting this yarn tied up in knots. Remember, the final product is a perfect ball of yarn with no kinks. No dimension can move forward until it's entire existence has reached this level of perfection because, we are all connected and as individuals we must all move together as a whole. Those of us who refuse to accept this process will be the ones to turn, resist, and tangle this yarn. Eventually, to release these tangles, the yarn has to be cut and reattached, pulled, or straightened out at different points. It will not be a smooth transition in any way, but a transition that has to be done. This mergence of our human existence is starting to take place right now, and we need to decide what individual roles we will play in this engagement.

I was once given a wonderful astrology reading, as a birthday gift, which confirmed and provided me with more clarity regarding this mergence. Yes, even us psychics, like to get a reading every now and then, and compare notes. This woman, using just my birth date and time, mentioned something in the first half of the reading which made me aware that this mergence was indeed a reality. She said I had a very strong psychic energy cycle, but then she mentioned that I represented what future human evolution will be. When I asked her for clarity she simply smiled and said, "Your ability to tap into spirit and angelic consciousness at will, is what we humans must learn to do with ease in order to adapt to the faster energy vibrations entering our planet."

Now obviously, this does not mean that in order for all of us to go through this transition of mergence with ease and clarity, we all need to become psychics! What it does mean, is that we need to start accepting the possibilities of spiritual existence with more openness. This will allow our mind and soul to co-exist between the two worlds without fear, anger, or lack of trust. So many people believe in the idea that we have Guardian angels or, that angels in general do exist. A recent poll showed that almost seventy five percent of people were open to the possibility of angels existing.

The amazing thing is that only a small portion of these people have ever experienced an angelic event or encounter, to warrant their belief. The pure level of faith in believing that a force greater than ours can watch over us, was enough for them to hold onto as a real basis for their existence. This pure level of belief or faith, is the door which allows us to begin coinciding with the acceptance of a higher vibration and intellectual awakening. Our angels say that the more we open to higher possibilities, the more we allow our conscious mind to take in a higher understanding of information, which are common to the level of existence in the spirit state.

This mergence is right now in it's infant stage. This change in energy and the fact that the planet is revolving faster is being introduced in a very subtle manner. It is being felt more in the emotional and mental bodies than the physical. It is not as though you are walking down the street and you feel an urge to hold on to the lamp post because the speed of the planet is throwing off your ability to walk straight. Even though it is subtle it is also very powerful and direct. In order to fully integrate, we as humans, need to make some changes in our lifestyle.

One strong area of change which has already been discussed in this chapter is the change in awareness. The ability to open your mind and stop taking things for granted. Realize we use a very small percentage of our brain's capacity. Do you think God would have created a brain with more potential if it was not destined to be used at one point or another? We have to start discovering the full potential of our mind. We cannot just settle and use the minimum amount of our brains just to survive. Incorporating tools such as meditation, exercise, proper nutrition, understanding karmic responsibilities from past lives, establishing communication with our spiritual helpers, and learning to listen to our body's demands, all need to become second nature to us. These are the tools which will assist us in adjusting to this mergence as well as guide us in avoiding further damage to our physical bodies and planet.

Working with new levels of healing modalities will become easier as we realize, once and for all, that we have greater control of our body and energetic fields. Developing a sensitivity to listen to our inner selves will also be essential. We are constantly in communication with our higher self, as well as our spiritual helpers, but we rarely pay attention to it. Our angels describe our higher self as that part of our thinking process that has access to higher dimensional information. This information provides us with insights, which assist us on our journey. We are in such a hectic pace that we do not have time to sit down and listen to our thoughts and ideas. We have been told to ignore the chatter in our heads, because there is too much to be done, and no time to do it. We also need to listen to each other instead of just hearing each other's voices. We are all teachers for one another. Once again, we are programmed by society to focus on our internal goals and plans, not realizing that many of these goals and plans cannot materialize without the help of others. Our angels constantly provide answers, insights, and ideas through other people that are placed in our path. A statement from your neighbor, the newspaper boy, or grocery clerk can be a message that your angel wants you to hear to assist you in moving forward with an obstacle in your life. Nothing is ever coincidence, and the sooner we start paying attention to all the little things which play out in our lives, the sooner we can get on track with our goals and missions. Opening to all this information will allow us to realize just how much help is being placed in front of us on a daily basis. This heightened level of listening and awareness, will help us in this transition, and allow us to be the ones moving forward during this mergence. Ironically, we need to slow down our ability to filter information, in order to catch up to the higher speed of our evolution.

Allow me to provide an example I had in a reading which deals with this subject of mergence. This woman came to see me one morning and seemed very nervous. She had never sought a psychic for advice, and her religious background added a level of guilt to the experience.

She described herself as a challenged Catholic who was forced to carry certain family religious traditions. After graduating from a well known Catholic college and moving forward in her life, she felt a certain uncomfortable hold that her religion and family had over her. She was constantly told by her family to follow certain guidelines set forth in her religion, and felt that God was going to punish her for being in my office. After ten minutes of calming her and assuring her that the devil was not going to enter my office and swallow her away, she finally eased a bit and felt more willing to speak freely. Many times I ask my clients what is the main reason or purpose in their desire to connect with their angel. Since I can only hold the angel's energy for a set amount of time, I want to make sure I know what area of their life I need to push the angel into, before I lose my connection. I also do this to allow my clients to understand that I am also there to listen to them with compassion, and not strictly to bypass them or their needs and rush their session.

This woman mentioned that she had seen me on a Spanish television show, in which I was introducing the subject of Guardian angels. I had demonstrated with several actors who came on stage, how I connected with their individual angels. She continued to tell me that she was running late to work but, could not peel herself away from this show. The more she listened, the more she wanted to understand or discover if this theory of Guardian angels was real. She always heard stories about angels in church and in the bible but, she was surprised hearing of someone that had regular encounters with them. When the show was over she found herself in tears, as she joined many of the audience members, guests, and crew who were also very emotional as the camera panned across the stage. She picked herself up from the couch, decided to call the television network, and find out more information about who I was, and how she could contact me. She said she normally would never do something so irrationally like this, but felt compelled to seek me out from an inner gut feeling.

She eventually tracked me down as was thrilled to find out I lived in the same city as she did, because the show was taped in Venezuela, and she though I lived in that country. After explaining how she tracked me down, she paused and looked at me shyly, and asked if I could help her find out who she was. I asked for some clarification to this question, and she said that her whole life she had lived under the veil of a proper Catholic woman, married, had a wonderful son, a full time job, but had no real clue as to the purpose of her existence. She had always feared God and would never question his ways. She accepted whatever God placed in her life for he always provided for her. At this age of thirty six, she felt she had no idea what her purpose was, had so many fears due to her religious upbringing, and felt her only push in life was to watch over her son.

This is a classic case of someone suffering instead of merging with this new level of higher awareness and consciousness. She had reached a point where life was no longer important for her sense of self and had become extremely depressed. She felt she had no worthwhile mission and worst of all, had no connections to anything in life, besides her son. Her career, religion, and marriage were simply activities which she used to spend her time in this existence. She had lost all desire to laugh, did not like her job, felt she could not relate to her husband, and eventually confessed that if it wasn't for her son, she had no reason to live. Once again, as I mentioned before, those individuals that cannot relate to this new vibration will lose their desire to exist and question their motive to live.

Upon finishing our reading, this woman was in tears, and looked as though she had dropped twenty pounds of stress from her shoulders. Her angel shared many details of her life which proved to her she was never alone and was being guided. She was given information that spanned from her childhood to her present day. This woman felt so relieved to understand that God was not going to punish her for coming to visit me, for missing Sunday service a few times, or for not wanting to follow all the strict guidelines of her religion. She was told about all the little things she did for others outside of the church which mattered much more. I also explained to her that religion was a group experience, while spirituality was a personal adventure or journey, which was open every day of her life, in or outside of a church. She began to see her life in a different perspective, gave herself permission to possibly change careers, to find one more emotionally satisfying. She also realized how much time was spent trying to be the perfect mother and wife, instead of just enjoying herself with her husband and son. Most of all, she had stopped doing all the enjoyable things she liked such as playing the piano, going to visit her friends, reading, and meditating, because she felt knowledge not provided directly by God or the bible was not pure knowledge. I told her the bible has incredible worthwhile information, but there is also a great deal of information in the day to day world we live in.

This woman was a completely different person when she left my office, than she was when she entered. As she left she said, "Thank you so much for allowing me to know it is OK to be myself, and wanting to enjoy my life is not a sin." She wiped the last few tears from her eyes and added, "From now on, my tears will be for the joy of rediscovering myself, learning more about the vastness of God's love, and working on ways to start communicating with my Angel." If others cannot love me for who I am and what I believe in, it will be there problem, and no longer my burden!"

The energy around this woman had shifted dramatically, from the lost soul who entered my office, to the strong willed woman who left. She had merged with her higher consciousness and also with the higher vibration around her. She had given herself permission to accept this shift, and had begun to reap the good feelings it provided. The simple process of allowing yourself to believe in greater possibilities, is the first step in gaining access to this mergence. Our Angels do not want us to suffer or have to endure hardships because of this mergence. They wish for this transition to be one of free will, and they will assist us every step of the way.

FURTHER THOUGHTS AND IDEAS TO ASSIST YOU WITH THIS MERGENCE

1. You don't have to become a New Age guru, run away from home to live atop a mountain, or disconnect from all your materials goods, to walk into this mergence without difficulty. You have to allow yourself a chance to let go of some old beliefs and patterns, which no longer serve purpose in your life. You have to be brave enough to follow your heart's desires, and not solely depend on your logical linear thinking to survive.

2. Feel free to explore other modalities of healing internally as well as externally. Understand your total self, not only the conscious part you are aware of on a daily basis. Be open to your dreams, trust

your intuitions, investigate your past lives, and be open to angelic communications available to all of us.

3.Dedicate time for self growth by meditating, or going to a special place, where you can release stress and negative patterns which have been accumulated. Question your motives in life and, see if what you are doing in life is serving yourself, humanity, or your soul. Be brave and make changes which you feel might increase your potentials. Go out of your way to find a sense of purpose and healing with the planet and others as well. Where can your services be of the highest and best good for the positive flow of love in this world? Realize we all have different beliefs, and they all serve a purpose at one point or another. Respect the differences in others, but find the time to discover your own truth. Seek the best in other people's opinions and put yourself in other's shoes from time to time. Knowledge is an incredible asset but, it goes nowhere, without having the experience to go with it.

4.Question your values and question if they serve who you are, or what others think you should be. Whenever you feel trapped inside, break loose, call time out, and seek possibilities and solutions. Realize this mergence is a positive experience, and not meant to destroy or burden you. It will help you discover all your potentials, and it can only lead you to a better more fulfilled existence. Know you are valuable to yourself and others that you encounter. Nothing is coincidence, so make the most of all the experiences placed in your path.

Chapter 10

Eighth Message: Group Consciousness

With the idea of mergence being implemented in the last chapter, we take this thought process one step further, and bring about the idea of group consciousness. As individuals, all of us have a great deal of influence, starting with the day to day activities in our personal lives, all the way to major decisions that we make which influence others. Individually, we make choices which affect how we manage our day to day schedule. On a group factor, such as families or work environment, many of our decisions affect how others construct their lifestyles as well. Our angels feel we only see the end results of our day to day choices, based on the outcomes which we personally experience. Very rarely do we consider how these choices or actions affect those around us, our community, work area, or perhaps the world. Many people feel that they serve no purpose, or play no role in other people's lives on a daily basis. The angels say we would be very surprised at just how much influence our existence plays out on everyone that crosses our path.

The angels want us to understand the concept of group consciousness. Group consciousness, according to them, is basically the understanding that, as humans, we all have to focus on the same positives outcomes for all of humanity. If we can understand how we influence others daily, then we can understand how powerful and productive we can be, if we all work on the same goals together for each other instead of against each other. At this point, I would like to share a story that I use in some of my classes to illustrate how our daily actions affect those individuals around us.

There is a young man who is leaving his house to go to work one morning. He locks the door of his home, jumps into his convertible car, and heads towards his office. As he starts down the street he reaches into his pocket for his pack of cigarettes. Her takes out his last cigarette, and without too much thought, throws the empty box out his open car not caring where it lands.

About one mile from his office he realizes he is running a bit late and decides to speed up. As he steps down on the gas pedal heading near the next intersection, the light turns yellow. He is in a rush and decides to speed even more, and barely passes the light before it turns red to avoid further delay.

The young man finally arrives at the parking area of his office, lowers the car radio which was blaring out loud, pulls up the convertible top, and races inside to start his work day. Sounds like a normal and uneventful trip to work, doesn't it? Let us rewind this story and take a look at everything else involved in this sequence of events. We will pay attention to the same series of actions we discussed earlier but, add in other individuals as well.

First, let us rewind to the first scene, the young man entered his car, lit up his cigarette, threw out his empty box, and headed to work. The empty cigarette box landed on the lawn of one of his neighbor's homes. The owner of that house just so happened to be looking out her window when she saw the box land on her front lawn. She also noticed other papers and debris on her lawn, decided to get a plastic bag, and go pick up all the garbage. She began picking up the odds and ends she saw thrown about, and bent down to pick up the empty cigarette box. As she got closer to the box she saw something shining and glittering in the grass. As she got closer to it, she realized it was her gold earring which she had lost the week before. She was so happy to have found it and, suddenly remembered that her daughter was coming over this morning to take her to the jewelry store to find a replacement.

She ran inside the house, called her daughter, told her she had found her earring, and said there was no need for her to take off from work and take her shopping. Her daughter advised her she had already asked for the time off from work, so she would just stay home and handle some bills that her piled up. This woman's daughter hung up the phone and began looking at her bills, trying to decide which ones had the most priority. As she scanned through the bills, she realized her electric bill was past due, and today was the deadline to pay to avoid interruption of service. She was so happy her mom had cancelled because now she had the time to go pay the bill and avoid a major problem.

Next, we go back to the second scene in the story in which the young man sped up at the intersection, and took the yellow light to avoid being late for work. On the other side of the light was an elderly man, driving the opposite direction, who noticed this young man speeding. He was angry that some people would drive so carelessly with no regards for others. As he thought about this even more, he thought that this young man could have created an accident for himself or someone else. Taking this chain of thoughts even further, he remembered that his brakes were acting up, he decided to change his course from the grocery store, and headed out to the mechanic instead. After a careful inspection of his brakes, the auto mechanic advised him he was very close to having a serious problem with his brake pads, and could have been in a situation soon where his brakes would have failed. The elderly man was relieved that he had made the decision to check his brakes instead of going straight to the grocery store.

Finally, we look at the scene where the young man arrives to the parking lot of his office, and goes inside to begin his workday. Well, it just so happens, that when he was pulling into his parking spot, a young woman was passing by on her way to work as well. She overheard the song playing on his radio, which was a bit loud, because his convertible top was down. She recognized the song right away because it was the wedding song chosen by her and her husband several years ago. That morning this young lady had a terrible fight with her husband and they both left the house in a bad mood. Hearing that song brought back memories of her wonderful wedding day, and she realized the argument that morning was petty, and their love for each other was much stronger. She quickly ran inside to call her husband. They talked for a few minutes, made up, and decided to meet at their favorite restaurant after work, and work things out.

Now, doesn't that young man's ride to work seem a great deal more important when you consider the chain of events and the changes it created for others. If we take this idea even further, all the people involved, the neighbor, her daughter, the elderly man, and the young woman all would continue this ripple effect of events and changes as they finished their daily routines. Many more changes would have been created by these series of events. The neighbor's interactions for that morning, or the daughter who may have met someone else on the way to pay her electric bill, the elderly man who decided to make some financial changes after using the grocery money for brakes, and the young woman, whose better attitude at the office could have affected her work production. There is an infinite amount of possible events that could have been created due to the actions that this young man took on his way to work, even though he had no conscious awareness of it. Now can you imagine, if he consciously made day to day decisions, based on the idea that each action would affect the best and highest good of all those around him? This is where the theory of group consciousness comes in.

The angels advise us that if we can consciously all work, as earthlings, with the positive end results in our actions to benefit everyone, the end results would be astronomical. If we could separate division lines between faith, race, society levels, and beliefs, we could all benefit and avoid a great deal of suffering on this planet. If every single person, from the moment they woke up, went out of their way to create a positive change for someone else, we would have this endless chain of fruitful outcomes on a daily basis. All of us are given this incredible tool known as the mind to function in areas of creativity, decision making, and free will. As individuals, we are taught throughout history to develop this mind for our individual gain. We focus a great deal on who we are, what our name is, where we live, what type of job we hold, and what level of society we fit in. We have created a world where individualism plays a major role in identifying who we are. As soon as you meet someone you exchange your names, possibly give some background details as to your profession, where you live, and maybe exchange a few more details of individual status and accomplishments, before the conversation ends. We have become a world of titles, brands, classifications, and code numbers to represent who we are as human beings.

Our Guardian angels do not have names or titles which they use to greet or associate themselves. So many people who come to see me for readings cannot wait to find out what their angel's name is, so when I explain the situation, they are somewhat disappointed. Our angels do not use names among themselves for communication. You will never hear one angel in the Angelic realm scream out to another, "Hey Mary, how are you?", "OK, Robert, are you working on anything special today?." They simply use a universal energy of love to greet one another. They have a telepathic form of communication in which they interact thoughts and messages back and forth. There is no need to individualize their existence for they know they are all equal and one with the God Source.

In the angel readings that I provide to my clients, the angels realize that we, as humans, are accustomed to addressing individuals with names. The angel will therefore provide me with a name which they want the client to associate them with. Most of the time, when I tell them the name the angel has chosen, it turns out that the name has a particular connection with them. It might be their favorite name, the name they wanted to give to their first child if that came about, or the name of a loved one who they truly admired. When these angels speak to me I receive a warm loving vibration, which enters my heart, and suddenly I am connected with paragraphs of information, various emotions, and corresponding images. The strange thing is that even though I am only seeing one angel in front of me, I feel as though the information is being provided by a group force. To a certain degree our angels have already mastered this understanding of group consciousness, in which they individually assist all of us on this planet, yet they still maintain an overall conscious game plan to assist us as a whole.

Among themselves, our angels are all equal loving creatures of light and love, they have no need for individual distinction. They recognize and respect the hierarchies of other angels they interact with, but overall, see themselves as a unit of total loving expressions. The higher you climb the level of various dimensions, which connect back to the Source, the less the need for individual identity. This is where group consciousness plays out more efficiently and has more productivity. We are on this planet on the very first initiation of trying to establish this sense of group consciousness and, have not yet touched the surface. We have not even entered the level of pre-kindergarten. What we have to learn is to release some of this individuality, and start focusing on how we, as a whole, can better our planet and bring about the resources for all of us to continue existing in harmony. When we hold on to this individualism or "I" identity, we become less connected with the needs of others, and this allows for selfishness to be an important factor in our decision making abilities. As we die and enter the spirit realm, we finally begin to see the effects of a higher dimension, in which harmony and peace are derived from a different form of existence. When we go into even higher dimensions we begin to see how this "I" identity begins to lose it's grasp on our thinking patterns.

One example of my first connection with this group consciousness, at a higher dimension, was when I was in my early twenties. As a young man, confused about my psychic abilities, I was constantly looking for resources or groups which would assist me in understanding some of my strange experiences. I finally found and joined a group that met once a week to develop and understand psychic phenomenon. At this point in my life, I felt like Dorothy, finally finding the land of Oz, and the Wizard. I so much wanted to be surrounded with people who had certain gifts like me, and that encouraged me to develop them. After a few weeks of working and developing my skills, I was introduced to the psychic activity known as channeling.

Channeling involves the ability of a psychic or medium, to allow an entity to speak directly through them, within the realm of their physical body. In other words, their body becomes a tool of communication, which the entity will use to transmit information.

Messenger for the Guardians

Some of the members of the group I joined were mediums and had done some channeling before. They had mentioned to me that a particular spirit guide or teacher, which they decided to call Odyssey, had tried several times to enter their bodies to provide some insights but none of them were strong enough to hold his energy. They were able to get messages from him using the Ouija board. The strange thing about Odyssey was that the few times someone did hold his energy for a few seconds, or even the times he came through on the Ouija board, his first words were always,

"We are here." I found it so strange that if he was a single being why would he always address himself as we. It was explained to me that he was from a higher dimension, in which they shared a sense of group thought. So here it was, my first introduction to group consciousness. This entity had never incarnated in a human form. I know many of you are now saying, "OK, I was doing fine with this angel idea but now things have gotten a bit too strange!" I just ask that you keep an open mind in understanding the possibility that other levels of consciousness exist besides the human race, the spirit world, and angels. Odyssey is a collaboration of a group consciousness from a higher dimension, which has decided to offer assistance to us in the avenues of health, love, and the understanding of advanced communication. He is a loving source of energy and information, who has become one of my strongest helpers during my life. You see, I was the only one in the group who was able to eventually channel, and maintain his energy for lectures, and guidance to us all. Till this day, he still connects with me, but not as frequently as in the past.

Through Odyssey, I learned the value of individuals working together for a common goal. I also discovered that power magnifies when minds join together to create a conscious flow of healing and communication. He taught me to see the overall picture in all decisions I made, while realizing how my actions would affect even those I was not in contact with. To this day, I am grateful to Odyssey for assisting me in removing many of my doubts and fears, as I grew into manhood with the development of a psychic energy. He has evolved into a higher dimension, which has made it more difficult for me to have regular contact with him, but at times will lower his energy to provide me with some needed information about myself, my development, or our planet.

We are being strongly urged by our Guardian angels to begin the baby steps in developing a new level of group consciousness on this planet. We need to stop separating ourselves in so many different categories and, realize we are all inhabitants of this planet. We must work together to maintain a form of balance and avoid self destruction. We need to start incorporating some of the tools discussed so far in this book, and realize that we can change for the better, but it cannot be done unless we are all on the same wavelength. Imagine if you started making some changes in your life, you passed some of the information you learn to someone else, and they also start changing. Eventually, we can be the proud parents of that first big baby step, in which we realize we can stand up by ourselves as a unit, as a whole, as a loving planet. If humanity can learn to focus together on resolving hunger, violence, housing, and providing to our children, we have a much better chance of evolving and not dissolving.

We need to let go of the strength and power given to a select few, and see everyone as a crucial element to the decision making process. We allow a select few to make decisions for us, yet, do not take the time to vote or become involved in the issues that will affect our lifestyles. We get so caught up in distinguishing ourselves from others that we fail to see the common thread that binds humanity. If we begin seeing each other as equal parts of a perfect creation, then we can truly start living in wholeness, as the spiritual beings we were always meant to be. This group consciousness theory follows hand in hand with the mergence taking place, which we discussed in the previous chapter. As we get closer to the energies of the Spirit realm, we no longer will have a need for individual power and possessions, and we will lose the urge to control others. We struggle in our daily existence because, we are constantly trying to catch up with those we feel have more than us. This definition of "more", can be divided in various categories such as money, prestige, power, property, and even love or happiness.

We have been taught, especially in the United States, to constantly achieve and be number one. In order for someone to be number one, someone else has to become number two. The moment we think that we have the right to make someone else number two, we have lost the ability to see each other as equals. If everyone is fighting to become number one, eventually others begin to feel futile at even trying due to competition, and we create a level of little motivation. This is exactly what is happening today in our society. Many have chosen not to play the game, have allowed for a select few to fight their way to number one, simply agreed to follow the rules that these few have created, whether they believe in these rules or not. We become complacent and so do our abilities to speak up for ourselves. Eventually, we give up our "I" identity, for others to control or manipulate. Under the consciousness of group, we begin to realize that depending on each other is not only the power that makes the force greater, but it is also the energy flow, which allows us to start seeing each other as equals. Instead of constantly fighting each other, the resources are focused as one, in which no one has to be lacking. Our planet was created to have all the necessary resources to provide for everyone. We have to start respecting the planet and these resources, and work as one identity to provide for all. Now, this group consciousness does not mean that we all become robots, and we lose all levels of individualism. What it does mean is that we honor the differences in each other but work together to provide for one another.

 In closing this chapter, let me add that group consciousness will provide humanity with a way to survive, not only today, but for as long as it takes for all of us to evolve into the spirit realm. This shift in consciousness, which is playing out right now, will flow easier if we also initiate this level of group consciousness. This idea of group consciousness will not happen overnight. The negative energies such as fear, greed, jealousy, and envy to name a few, which have risen in our planet have to be removed. A more positive vibration has to be created for this process to work. Changes will be required in many areas of our societies. For example, hospitals working together with each other to avoid lack of rooms or care, individual State programs and legislatures combining their resources to work together, religions accepting their differences, and working on their similarities instead, and all of us taking that extra minute to help each other, must all start right now. Little steps being created now, such as neighborhood crime watch programs, serve as an introduction to becoming one within this group consciousness. Our angels say we need to develop this sense of oneness, and realize we are all renting space and time here on this planet, once we die our lease is over, no one really owns the planet. We will all gather again and rent some new spaces from lifetime to lifetime, and eventually do the same in higher dimensions.

Meditation to invoke Group Consciousness:

Enter a relaxed state of mind and body using the techniques discussed earlier. Take three deep breaths, each breath relaxing you more and more, allow your mind, body, and spirit to join as one. Repeat this several times until you find yourself physically reaching a state of relaxation. With your eyes closed, imagine you have a large candle in front of you. You light this candle and stare at the beautiful light which it emits in the room. If you have trouble visualizing, then go ahead and light a real small candle a few feet from you. See the brilliance of this light, feel the warmth it provides, and understand how it is also a source of clarity. Allow for the feelings for love which emit from your heart to go beyond your physical self, and enter this light from the candle. See it as a green healing light that gets stronger and stronger.

Next, imagine that your neighbor is doing this same exact meditation at the same exact time as you. Without getting up and looking outside your window, you will use your visualization and imagination to see and sense a beautiful green light being formed inside your neighbor's home. Take this idea one step further, and imagine everyone on your block is creating this loving green light in their homes as well. Now, you have rows of homes with beautiful green loving lights emitting through their windows as far down as you can see. Due to the many candles being lit at the same time you start to see a glow of light that surrounds the whole neighborhood.

Take this visual imagination even further and realize your whole community and city is actually doing this meditation, suddenly, gorgeous glows of green healing rays are lighting up the entire city, and the cities that follow. This provides you with such a wonderful feeling inside that you begin to float above your house maybe ten to fifteen feet. Now you see all the others with their individual lights also floating above their homes . All these lights begin to join and form as one beautiful glow. Instead of individual lights, all you see is one enormous glow of green healing light. This scene is so beautiful, it surrounds your heart with love, and these positive emotions lift you even higher and higher.

As you go higher, you now realize it is no longer just your city or the neighboring cities, but the entire planet has been covered in this beautiful green healing glow. You continue even higher and eventually see the entire planet engulfed in this beautiful energy. Now, you realize you are no longer your physical self, but an extension of this glowing light. You have become one with the candle, one with everyone else's candles, one with the planet. Everyone is experiencing the same sensations, and you can truly see the potential of love and harmony on this planet. You are experiencing group consciousness in all it's glory.

Take the time to experience and enjoy this sensation and slowly take three very long deep breaths. With each breath allow yourself to begin the journey of coming back down. Slowly, return from a floating sensation above the planet, back to your room. Know inside your heart, that with each day that passes by, one more house will join you in your meditation. Know that in the end we are all one already, we just need to show it to each other, and feel it on a conscious level.

Chapter 11

Ninth Message: Children

One of the most influential tools being bestowed upon our planet to assist us with all our changes, are the children. Many times, in so many readings, Guardian angels have told my clients to pay special attention to their children. Not all, but many of the children which have entered our planet over the last fifteen years or so, have come into this physical world with a different sense of awareness. At a young age, they have stepped on the stage and demanded attention. They wish to be heard and understood, because from infancy they are aware that they are special, and are here for a specific purpose. I refer to them as the soldiers of tomorrow, who have consciously decided to enter this planet at a time when humanity needs them the most. The latest new age buzz has labeled these children with the title "Indigo" or "Crystal". I simply refer to them as enlightened little ones, who have no time to play.

There seems to be two breeds of these children coming into this world. One breed comes in troubled, shortly after entering the material world. This group enters the planet with challenges, which begin to be exhibited soon after they are born. They are locked inside their own world of communication, can be very aggressive or violent, and overall, seem disappointed by their arrival upon this planet. Actually, according to our Guardian angels, that is exactly what is taking place. Many of these children are first time incarnates in human bodies. In Spirt, where limitations rarely exist, these brave earthly angels decided to bring their innocence into this world of negativity. Since they have never experienced the limitations of a physical body, they struggle from the onset. They have never had a previous past human life and find themselves trapped in a human existence which can be quite threatening compared to a spiritual body. This forces them to mentally withdraw, they feel a sense of imbalance, and this does not allow them to function as they did in Spirit.

This imbalance begins from the moment they find themselves within the constraints of the mother's womb. The soul feels restricted and begins to realize it has lost it's spiritual oneness or identity. As the months go by and the child gets closer to it's delivery date, this child's soul now wants to change it's mind and return to spirit, and analyze why it even decided to enter. By the time it can figure out what is happening, it is now being born, and the soul's lack of desire to participate in this physical world creates a mental breakdown. The irony is that the soul originally wanted to come in to this world and assist the planet in releasing the negativity it is producing. We have to remember, we do not consciously recall our life mission upon our entry into this world, thus, these innocent souls find themselves entering a dense negative planet with no clue why they are here! In many cases, upon entering the physical world, this child enters with complications such as weak immune systems, intellectual inadequacies, withdrawal, and a sense of rage and destruction. Some are labeled as autistic or having attention deficit disorders. Many of these symptoms are manifested by the time they are two or three years old. It is a trauma for these children to find themselves physically and mentally confined to the limitations of a human body. Many of these children do not outgrow these symptoms and end up in institutions or health care systems for a long portion of their lives. The good news is that the angels have told me that soon a level of recognition will be given to these children and certain programs, therapies, and energy work will allow them to release the initial disappointment they hold. With this assistance, they can get back into a normal lifestyle, both physically and mentally.

We have to remember that not all children who enter this world with these disorders are Indigo or Crystal. We are speaking of a very small percentage of these Indigo and Crystal children who manifest these disorders. Other children who do have these disorders have unfortunately been hit with cellular problems, parents who had chemical dependencies during or before their birth, genetic defects, and certain levels of mental retardation are also some reasons why some children do exhibit complications upon entering our world. One of the reasons for the name "Indigo" to label these children is in direct connection to the color of the aura which surrounds a good portion of these children's body. We all have an auric field of energy around our body which holds various colors. In these children, the main color is Indigo.

The second breed of children are the ones who have also decided to enter this world with a strong mission, but are not taken aback by their limitations. When I speak of limitations, I am referring to the difference between existing in spirit form and in a physical form. In spirit you can move anywhere simply by thought, you manifest things at a faster rate, and have a great deal more conscious information about the functions you are performing. These children enter this world with certain characteristics and traits, and usually most parents are at a lost in finding ways to communicate with them. The parents tend to feel inadequate, because these children bring about certain questions at a young age, which they have no responses for. The reason for this is that these children are consciously aware of their inner purpose or life mission at an early stage, and do not want any outside interference. They have an attitude of, " *Get out of my way, I have things to learn and do",* and find it very annoying to be delayed or slowed down in their growth. From what the angels have shared with me regarding these children, I will attempt to provide some insights and character traits to assist parents who are at a lost. I will describe in more detail how these children react, function, and go about accomplishing their goals as we go further in this chapter. There are also many wonderful books about Indigo children available, which can also provide guidelines for the many confused parents.

These children are basically the future evolution of this planet's inhabitants. As I mentioned in the chapter discussing mergence, the planet has shifted and adults are having a hard time wanting to stay and function on this new shift. To offset this imbalance, these children are coming into this world to replace many of the souls who are calling it quits, and to educate the ones that are willing to adapt. All of us enter this world with a veil, which somewhat shades the clarity as to our life mission or purpose. These children have a much thinner veil, giving them more clarity as to what they need to focus on from an early age. They usually become frustrated and misunderstood because they feel too much time is wasted in non-productive manners or activities. They do not wish to follow the so called normal procedures or steps required for small children to grow, enter, or contribute to society.

Many of these children have the following traits or characteristics in common:

1. They hate being told what to do and will let you know that from the very beginning. They seem bothered that their parents would even dare to try and teach them because they actually came here to teach the adults.

2. They are extremely intelligent from an early age, and get bored very easily. Their mind's capacity is very vast, and performing tasks over and over is useless. They need new challenges, and want to resolve problems differently than from the way they are instructed.

3. They are also extremely logical and technical, and the idea of a three year old operating a computer, is very common for these children.

4. They want to be talked to like adults, not like children. In other words, they want clear and concise explanations as to why certain things happen, why they are restricted from doing things, and why they are not allowed in adult conversations. The response that they cannot do something because daddy says so is not good enough!

5. They hold a high level of spiritual consciousness, and often find themselves offering advice and wisdom by the age of four or five to their friends and parents.

6. They are naturally born with the desire to be among people and not isolated. The have a strong inclination to assist humanity, associate and be around older people instead of playing with children their own age, and seem interested in worldly events. Sometimes they are diagnosed at school as being antisocial, because they do not associate with the other children. In reality, they are bored with the other children unless they meet up with one of their own kind. Sometimes they are more entertained with their own imagination and abilities than what is being offered in their classroom.

7. These children are also very psychic, intuitive, and have the capability to communicate with their angels and other beings from the spirit realm. Many will tell their parents that they see their angel walking around, or describe a relative who died before they were born. It is normal for them to have vivid dreams, which are prophetic or that contain memories of their existence in a previous life or spirit state.

8. They are natural caretakers, usually are the first ones to run and get a bandage if someone has a cut, or wish to take care of their younger siblings when they are ill. They can heal others as soon as they can walk and talk. They have the capacities to increase their energies, and change the physical or emotional moods of others.

By the time these children reach the age of ten to twelve they will feel that school is a waste of time, and they can learn more by themselves with computers and books. The sad thing is that they are right. They are also very inclined to share or give away everything they have such as toys, clothes, or books, even if they are new, with no remorse. These soldiers are basically the new generation of individuals who have a head start on the level of consciousness we, in this planet are trying to achieve. They arrive already encoded with the changes required to live a productive life within this new shift we are encountering. They have the awareness and knowledge to assist us in moving from the three dimensional world, into the fourth and fifth dimensional existence awaiting us. Unlike these children, most of us are trying to change or reprogram ourselves to this level, while they already have entered with this added capacity. It is our duty and responsibility, according to our angels, to support and assist these children, as they adjust to exist and accomplish their mission in our union.

As parents to these type of children, many find themselves at a loss, confused, desperate, and even feel inferior to these little earth angels, that they have brought into this world. Some of these parents come to see me for a reading not because of their own personal problems, but because they want to find a solution which will allow them to be more connected with their child.

Parents are seeking ways to handle them, and ways to create avenues so that these children and themselves can meet halfway. They do not want their children to be stifled, they want them to express themselves easier, without the teachers or themselves going crazy. They also want to learn to understand their needs, discover their spiritual path, and sometimes wonder why they were the ones chosen to bring in these gifted children to our planet. Allow me to share a few stories from my experiences, and parents who are trying to deal with these special children.

One day while teaching an angel class at the college, one of my students wanted to know if it was permissible for her daughter to come to the last class, because she had no babysitter and really did not want to miss the class. Her seven year old was always talking about angels, and had even told her mother what her angel looked like on several occasions. I told her it would be fine. In that last class, one of the ending exercises I would do was to walk around the class and tune into some of my students' angels, and provide a brief message. I went ahead and did this for about fifteen or twenty minutes. I would describe the physical features of the persons' Guardian angel and give them a quick message. I decided to take a break and give the class a few minutes for recess. During that break

I overheard the little girl, who was just sitting there witnessing the events, turn to her mom and say " What is the big deal, I already knew all those angels were standing there, I see them all the time!"

Another example of these wondrous little beings comes from a client I had. This mother of two came to see me for a reading. She mentioned to me that one day she was in her bedroom and her children were playing and watching televison in the living room. She had just finished reading a book about positive affirmations and statements that can bring about changes in your life. She decided to try out one of the exercises in the book. This exercise involved going into a meditative state, and saying over and over a statement, which had to deal with a specific outcome that they wanted in their life. So she went into deep relaxation, and inside her head she began saying over and over, "I want protection and good health for my children." She was doing this for close to ten minutes when suddenly her little five year old girl came running into the room and screamed out, "Mommy, stop worrying so much about us, we're going to be just fine." Her daughter gave her this look, insinuating that she was bothered that her mom was wasting time focusing on them, when she should be focusing on other issues.

On a separate occasion, a mother shared with me that she was having many problems with her little boy in pre-kindergarten. Apparently he would get bored, not stay still, and constantly wanted to be talking. On one particular day, the teacher decided to give everyone a test, to end the last half hour of the class. Ten minutes into the test this little boy walked away from his desk, and started talking to all the other children about the classroom. When the teacher told him to sit down and finish his test, he responded by saying he was already finished, and was walking around to see if any of the other children needed help! The teacher had no other resolution, but to just sit back and smile at this little child. Even though he was not deliberately trying to create problems, this little child was bored, and felt it was his duty to assist the rest of the class.

There is one particular book which I recommend to those parents which feel they are dealing with one of these special children. It is called "Indigo Children", by Lee Carroll and Jan Tober. It is an excellent, and resourceful book, which explains these children in more detail, and also gives things to look for to evaluate your child's progress. The book also provides ways to assist them as they get older. I also strongly recommend this book to teachers who work with children from the ages of three to ten. As I mentioned earlier, the color indigo is a representation of the primary color, which energetically surround these children. Indigo is also the color associated with one of our body's energy center known as the Third eye. This is the energy center known as a Chakra, where we create our psychic intuitive energy, and is located between the eyebrows. I found this subject of Indigo and Crystal children to be so important, that I even started creating some workshops at the college to assist parents, and these children as well.

The difference between an Indigo child and a Crystal child is simply in their personality. They both have the same abilities and come into this world with similar missions. The Crystal child is more tolerable and easier to work with, than the Indigo, at times.

Now, many parents who hear about these special children automatically feel left out if their little boy or girl does not fit into this category. Sometimes, they come to me during a lecture and say, "I know my child is an Indigo child, he is so bright." This may or may not be the case, but I stress that parents should not take this idea to use as a social tool to separate themselves from mothers who have normal everyday loving children. These Indigo children are few and in between, and our angels stress that this does not mean we ignore the other higher population of children also entering our world. All children entering are eventually going to be in charge of running this planet when they get older. All children need to have the highest level of love and support to assist them throughout their lives.

On many occasions I have visited family or friends who share with me, stories about their children playing with imaginary playmates. They are comfortable with the idea, because they know they will eventually grow out of it. The funny thing is that on many of these occasions, I have sat down to play and talk with these children and also have seen their so called imaginary friends, who turn out to be their angels or spirit guides. Children are the resources for our future. Whether they are part of this Indigo generation or not, it is our responsibility to help them open their minds to their highest potential, bring them various levels of knowledge, and not just the ones we hold as truth for ourselves. More importantly, we need to start listening to them, for they have valuable information to share with us, information which can assist us in adapting to the new changes ahead of us. We need to make them feel loved and wanted for they will need a strong support system to deal with the future plans of this planet. In today's time, there is so much anger in our teenagers. We have become too preoccupied with our own needs as adults that we are not finding time for the children. Many of these teenagers have working parents who in order to survive, just cannot find the time to spend with them, and they are retaliating with abusive language, actions, and a sense of selfishness. I cannot wait for the day when meditation and a certain level of spirituality, not necessarily religion, is taught to all children at a grade school level. I feel we need to start showing children that they have a lot more tools they can use to adapt to life then just the ones taught at a curriculum level.

As a closing statement for this chapter, I ask that all parents or parents to be, who are reading this book, to take the time to truly be a parent. This is a lifetime job, one with many hardships, but unlimited amounts of rewards as well. I was given the blessing to be a father during the last stage of writing this book, and have witnessed both the hardships and joys. It is truly not an easy task, but it is one that if done with pure love, will bring about some of the most rewarding memories you can possibly imagine.

Exercises and games to play with children to expand their minds:

With this new breed of children arriving on our planet, and their strong desire to know more, express more, and share more, I have included some simple games and exercises which parents can incorporate to enhance their abilities.

1. Seeking game: Hide an object in the house and have the children try to guess where it is without physically moving about the house. Have them use their imagination and visualization to go around the house in their minds, and see if they find the object. This allows their mind to expand beyond the limited abilities of their senses.

2. Picture telepathy: Grab a magazine or illustrated book and focus on a visual image, and have the children try to guess either the shape, color, or image you are staring at. This exercise allows the children to use other levels of communication within the mind which is non- verbal.

3. Problem solving: Bring into their environment, any and all types of problem solving games, puzzles, or computer programs where they are forced to discover various solutions to one problem. This activates their creativity and teaches them to think outside the box.

4. Animals: These children work extremely well with animals, and are natural born healers as I mentioned before. Providing them with pets assists them in their nurturing values, as well as responsibility. Many of these children will enter professions where they will be responsible for assisting and nourishing others.

5. Allow them to participate: Once again children are very intuitive. Feel free to have them participate in minor decisions around the house. Ask for their opinions, and allow them to feel as important role models within the family structure. Teach them to discover their leadership at a young age.

6. Meditation: Children love to use their imagination and creativity to an extreme. Teach them to join you in your meditations. Have them do deep breathing exercise and release stress. Just because they are young, does not mean that they are not dealing with difficult issues and stress. Realize many of these children are overloaded with information and need an outlet.

7. Spiritual Values: Feel comfortable speaking to children about angels, and ask for their input and experiences as well. Realize they have just recently arrived from the Spirit realm, and unlike most of us, are still consciously connected to much of that level.

8. Expression: Allow these children to write and express their feelings. Take the time to listen to their stories whether they are real or made up. They are here as communicators, and will be changing resources for the future through their actions and words. They might seem young, but they have arrived with a great deal of information to share. Lately, I have seen articles in the newspaper where young children under the age of twelve have managed to write and publish their own books.

Chapter 12

Tenth Message: Love

We now enter one of the areas of messages from our angels which applies to every single human being on this planet. This area of discussion is the universal vibration of love. All of us are either looking for it, trying to hold onto it, suffering because of it, or trying to take it to a higher level. Love is the universal energy source for all that is. It is the life source of all dimensions, the glue that keeps all emotions intact, and the umbilical cord which connects all of us to our God Source.

In this chapter, we will focus on information regarding the topic of love from our angels' point of view, in it's relation to three areas. These three areas include love of self, love of humanity/relationships, and spiritual love. We have received messages from the beginning of time from many different sources regarding this topic. The Bible is loaded with examples in which angels are portrayed as messengers of love. I will attempt to simply the understanding of the love that emits from the God Source, which permeates through all that is. I also hope to explain the unconditional love that exists from our Guardian angels to us. Realize that love is an experience capable of creating so many changes and bringing about so many emotions. Love has been the element which started wars, and separated groups of people from one another. It has also been the element that molded groups together and created bonds between nations. It has been the inspiration for ideas, artistic masterpieces, endless romantic songs, and the fuel to conquer obstacles. Let us begin by first understanding the concept of self love.

One of the most difficult aspects for humans, according to our angels, is the achievement of self love. As individuals, we become engulfed with the idea of pleasing others from a very young age. In many religions, we are taught to love and honor our God Source as well as our parents, and one another. As soon as we learn to rationalize, we begin to seek our parents' approval and love, in order to be accepted or rewarded. Society teaches us that we must be good to others and love our brothers and sisters, our neighbors, and at times our enemies. Very little time is spent to teach us to love ourselves. The Indigo children, which we discussed in the previous chapter, do not bring this lack of self love into their being. They are aware of their self worth and importance from the start, and try not to depend on others to satisfy their own self recognition. Many would think that this also brings in a level of arrogance and selfishness, but in actuality, it removes unnecessary obstacles from their paths.

In many sessions with my clients and their Guardian angels, I have had the repetitive message expressed that they needed to love themselves more. They tell us that love is the only constant energy force which exists on this planet. What that means is that love is the only variable in any equation, and that will always be constant. It is accessible to each and every person at any time upon this planet. Self love is the first accessible level of love which exists the moment we are born. Unfortunately, it is also the first accessible level which many of us fail to connect with.

Many of us struggle to be accepted by others, and in that struggle we seek faults to serve as excuses for not being wanted or accepted. We struggle at various points in our lives with the other different levels of love, such as love of family, love of friends, exploring intimacy, and seem lost and angry when these loves are not reflected in our everyday life. We will spend lifetimes searching and seeking these loves, yet, we do not take as much time or spend as much effort, in discovering self love. At a young age many of us are confused to explore or express love, and we feel that this love is an interaction between two different people. We fail to realize that the first true love is the interaction between yourself and your soul.

Love enters our existence in many different stages according to our maturity and physical development. The moment we are born we depend on our parents to nurture, love us, and take care of us, as we adapt to the awkwardness of the physical body we have been given. As we reach the age of six, we are thrown into society where we need to battle for the attention and love of our teachers and other family members such as siblings and grandparents. When we reach our teenage years, we feel a need to stop depending on our parents as much, and we try to seek a romantic level of love from others in society within our age group. From that point forward it turns into a lifetime struggle to hold and discover a loving relationship with a mate, and then with our own children. Throughout this whole cycle little time is dedicated to loving yourself, and appreciating yourself for who you are.

Still to this day as I have mentioned, one of the top questions I receive from my clients to their angel is,"Can my angel tell me who my soulmate is, and when I will meet them?" For some reason, we relate to the word love as an attraction for another being or thing. We fail to see the possibility of loving ourselves as a relationship between our heart and soul, our conscious and subconscious, our outer physical being, and our inner spiritual existence. There are many one on one relations within our own individual being which are screaming for love and recognition, but we are too busy seeking outside of ourselves. Our angels tell us that usually one of the reasons we feel we cannot find that perfect love in our lives, is because we have neglected one or more of our own internal love relations.

Our angels say, the ability for us to experience love as an everyday event, is all around us. We need to look around and within our boundaries, and discover what makes us happy. So many of us reach a point in our life that we start cutting back on things which used to bring us happiness because we lack the time. If not, we feel we need to devote all the possible free time to seek and create that perfect relationship, that continues to elude us. Things such as our talents, self acceptance, appreciation for natural beauty, laughter, and exploration begin to take space in the back of our minds as we focus more in the hunt for true love. When we can look at ourselves and appreciate our perfection, then we are ready to allow another soul to enter our hearts, and appreciate their perfection in union with our own. The angels tell us that we sometimes become spoiled with the unconditional love from the spirit realm we left behind, that we struggle trying to find something compatible in this material world. In Spirit, love simply is, it is all about us, and it does not have to be tapped into or created. In the physical plane it still simply is, yet we are blinded to it's accessibility because our energy is denser and slower. This slower energy allows us to create self made obstacles, which cloud the clarity of the love that exists all about us.

To give you an example as to how the lack of self love can destroy someone, allow me to share an experience in a reading I had with a woman in her early fifties. This woman basically wanted to talk to her Guardian angel, and scold him or her for not bringing love into her life. She was an attractive woman, financially secure, educated, and in control of her life, according to her. Her main complaint was that she never had a relationship which lasted. She had been divorced twice, and had basically given up on the idea that two people could actually love and be together for more than four years! I could feel the anger in her voice as she tried to explain to me all the horrible misfortunes she had experienced in the area of love. Like always, I try to allow my clients to speak and relax before I start my session, because I use their physical energy to connect with their angel. So, I allowed this woman to vent and speak from her heart for a few minutes before starting our session. Soon thereafter, I began to start connecting with her angel, and I noticed her tight lipped facial position and clenched fists across her lap.

After physically describing her angel to her, she quickly jumped in, and told me to ask her angel why he had failed to connect her with a perfect love mate. Her angel smiled, said it was not that he had failed, but rather she had failed to open her heart and mind to countless opportunities he had placed in her path. She became agitated with this response ,and was ready to start a debate. Her angel added that he wanted to hear what she felt about herself first, before he would go on explaining. Caught off guard, she stood up, and asked what he meant by this question. Her angel again repeated and asked, "How do you feel about yourself, your individual oneness?" He asked her if she loved herself. She quickly answered yes, very knowingly, and he asked her why. She looked at me a bit confused, and I simply told her that I was here in the middle as a translator, and that she needed to answer his question, so we could get on with the rest of the reading.

This woman stayed silent for about two minutes and began to cry. She said she never felt that she knew herself in her heart. She spent most of her life accomplishing goals and reaching levels of so called perfection in her life. She figured by doing this, her perfect mate would notice her above other women, and be drawn to her. Her angel smiled his typical angelic smile, which only they can truly master, and told her that when she was twenty one years old she met this young man in college who sat in front of her in her philosophy class. She stared up at the ceiling for a few seconds as she ran through her memory files. She said yes, he would always ask her questions about her personal life, and he always got on her nerves. Her angel continued, and asked if she remembered that he was the same man who offered to take her home when her car broke down in the school parking lot. She thought again for a few seconds and said yes, but wondered what did this have to do with anything!

Her Guardian angel asked her once again, why did she refuse to allow him to take her home, even though she found him attractive. Again, she said it was because he always wanted to know things about her personal life, which she felt was none of his business. She eventually changed her story, and admitted that she was upset that her car had broken down. She was embarrassed to accept his assistance or anyone else's, because in her perfect world, she should not have been driving a car with problems. She also added that his personal questions forced her to think about certain aspects of her personality and her life, that she hated. So this young man was forcing her to see herself for who she was, and this was an issue she did not want to deal with.

Her angel told her that he had a crush on her, but she was so detached from self love that he intimidated her from getting close to him. Her angel went on to give details of two other men who were placed in her life, and again because of issues dealing with lack of self love she created excuses and never gave them a chance. The angel told her that all the men she eventually dated or married were men who fell for her image of perfection, because they were impressed with what she represented and not who she was.

It was this same false impression she created for herself, which never allowed her to find someone to enter her heart on a permanent basis. In her inability to truly love herself and seek perfection, she had pushed away the men in her life who appreciated the total package. In addition to this, her ability to love herself for who she was went unexplored. Those men saw her total being, perfect or not, and would have spent a lifetime with her. They would have been willing to be a part of her life, if only she had given herself a chance to believe that who she was in the inside, was just as important as the person she was portraying on the outside. She wasted several opportunities to be with her soul mate.

Our ability to appreciate who we are as an individual allows us to grow into the full spiritual beings we are. Once this is achieved, we produce a high level of love for ourselves and what we do. This in turn creates a positive energy, and others are drawn to this energy. Giving ourselves a chance to accept our full essence in all aspects of our individualism creates a level of love, which pushes us to accomplish our life mission. This also removes the insecurities of waiting for others to approve of who we are or to teach us how to love. Self love is the seed which allows us as human beings to develop the ability to see the best in others as well. As we work through our fears, personal issues, and faults to develop self love we also allow ourselves to see the true love which exists in all other beings as well. This makes our lives a blessing rather than a chore which has to be completed.

The second area of love we will touch on is love for others. This is such a huge area of struggles and difficulties because of the fact that we all have different needs, personalities, desires, and characteristics. As I briefly touched in the beginning of this chapter, we go through periods of our lives where we begin to understand that love comes in a variety of possibilities as we open to the options placed before us. These options change as you mature and take on new responsibilities. You have your love of family members, love of friends, love of humanity in general, and of course, that special electrifying intimate love of your mate. Our parents play an important role in the development of love due to the fact that they represent our first role models in this area. We gain our first experiences of what love is by the interaction we receive from our parents the moment we are born.

Earlier in this book, I spoke about how as a child, affectionate embraces and hugs were not common experiences in the early years of my home surroundings. Therefore, as I grew older, I had difficulty in showing physical love. It was somewhat uncomfortable to embrace or hug someone as a sign of affection. I avoided hugs by friends, family members I had not seen in a long time, and especially total strangers. We are born seeking affection from the moment we open our eyes. That affection can be the warmth of the parent's body, the milk from the mother's breast, or just being cuddled and held by a proud parent. Even though I was provided with this type of affection, it was not demonstrated outside of me, by my parents to one another, or many of my family members. We hold on to this desire of receiving affection, especially by our parents, into our entire lifetime. What we do is hide it because by the time you are a teenager you are supposed to be independent, and not wish to be seen by your peer hugging, kissing, or holding your parents hands.

Our Guardian angels cannot believe what we go through in our lives just to connect with any aspect of love. They find it hard to believe that a feeling we long for so deeply in our hearts is also a feeling we try not to express due to rejection. This takes us back to self love and acceptance. If we love ourselves enough to appreciate our perfection, then we cannot have any room in our minds to allow someone else to connect us with rejection. Our angels are true romantics, they speak about our endless opportunities to touch someone else's heart, and see them float in the air as they walk away from us. They see love as such a beautiful form of expression that they cannot believe we struggle so much in this area of our lives. I had one Guardian angel ask me why, with millions of people living on this planet at the same time, and everyone wanting to have a love connection, why do so many of us go around alone and sad? I responded by saying that most people cannot find the right person to make them happy. The angel quickly responded by saying that if they were happy to begin with, they didn't need someone to make them happy, just someone to allow them to express their love. Needless to say, I lost the debate, yet it is so awesome to share back and forth with these beings of light and love, not because they have all the answers, but because they have unconditional love to accept all our responses with no judgement!

In general, most humans fall behind when it comes to unconditional love for others. We are quick to judge things that are different from us. Once again this is where fear brings it's ugly face into the picture. If we feel someone else is different, or has different ideas than our own that automatically makes us feel that they will not agree with who we are. If they do not agree with who we are then we assume they will try to force us to change, and before that happens we will push them away or ignore them. We fear they might change or force us to change our own opinions of who we think we are. Fear will stop you from changing as we talked about in the first few chapters of this book. So bottom line, we have difficulty in expressing love to others due to the fear that they might force us to see ourselves differently, or force us to deal with rejection. Again, if we are forced by someone else to see who we really are, we are not ready for that challenge, we go back to the first love difficulty, which is self love.

Our angels want us to learn that the differences within all of us is what allows us to learn more about ourselves. How else can we discover more about our existence as an individual if we do not see the things that makes us different. If we all think, act, and look the same, we have no comparison to create changes and uniqueness. The ability to change our life based on experiences encountered in love of others is one of the tools we have to gain clarity into our existence and our life mission. If we can master this process, we do not have to repeat so many physical lives, and we can move towards our spiritual evolution at a much quicker pace. Love of others, regardless of the type of relationship involved, also allows us to grow as spiritual beings. This planet is the testing area where we discover how much further we need to prosper, and how much we still have to learn about ourselves to reach that unconditional level of universal love. Sometimes the fear of your love not being accepted, or the overall inability to express love, can cast a blockage that will carry from one lifetime to another. Below is an example of such a situation.

During a reading one day, a woman's Guardian angel showed me several scenes from her most recent past life. At the age of twenty-four, back in the early 1800's, she was married to a man who was chosen for her by her family. She had no love for this man, but in her family tradition this pre-arranged marriage was a normal process. Six months into the marriage, she ran away from her husband because she could no longer stand living in a false relationship. She feared returning to her parents' home, for this would dishonor them. Her only other alternative was to go as far away from her community as possible, by herself. She had a difficult journey for women in those days did not travel alone, and the few that did were looked upon as low class or prostitutes. Several towns later, she found a place where she felt she could start her life anew. Maybe here she could find a man she could truly love and possibly have a child she so wanted. After several months, she found herself working as a seamstress and becoming self sufficient. She eventually found a man who fell in love with her, with the same intensity she had for him. She never mentioned her past to him, for that memory was a stain in her heart, and she wanted to forget that marriage all together. She wanted to marry this new individual, become pregnant, hold her child in her arms, and simply put her past to rest.

Time passed and she did marry this gentleman, but was unable to get pregnant. Eventually she gave up on the idea of being a mother. She figured that God had punished her for abandoning her first husband and disobeying her parents wishes. As more years passed, she became angrier and depressed, and began ignoring her husband, who she initially looked upon as her true love. Eventually, he lost patience with her, and had an affair with another woman. He decided to move in with this other woman because she was able to bare him a child. Now alone and miserable, she gathered all her inner anger, hatred, and disappointments, and went outside her home late one night. She looked up at the night sky and yelled at God with all her might. She told God she did not need his approval, his love, or his protection. She added that she did not need anyone in her life, she did not need love to survive, and could live by herself without having to depend on anyone.

Several years later this woman passed away due to malnutrition, very lonely, and bitter. What happened though, was that her entry into the Spirit realm was a difficult one. She held on to the anger and bitterness, but more importantly she held on the words she screamed at God, when she was still alive. Unable to release this anger completely, she re-entered into her present life with those vibrations still intact. That emotional energy of refusing to accept love, was so powerful that in her current life, she lost her parents to a car accident at the age of four. She was raised by her grandmother until the age of nine. At that point, her grandmother suffered a heart attack, lost her life, and she was placed in an orphanage. She left the orphanage at the age of twelve, and was raised by foster parents whom she never really got along with. She suffered throughout her life, and now at the age of twenty-four, she had come to see me because she had been married for three years, had two miscarriages, and so badly wanted to be a mother.

Her angel explained to her that her anger from her past life, and it's energy, had carried over to this present life. She requested to God, in her past life, that she needed no one in her life to survive. Those words carried over, and from her early years she was constantly alone, and those who did love her were constantly removed from her life, to fulfill her request. This woman cried and truly understood her feelings from her past life, and felt a weight removed from her heart. She stated that in this life she never really felt loved, and had no love for herself. She was surprised that the man she was with had enough of an interest in her, to even marry her.

This same woman called me about a year and a half later to let me know she was holding her newborn daughter in her arms, and just wanted to thank me for allowing her angel to assist her in releasing her anger towards love. The wonderful thing about uncovering past life traumas is that, our minds are so powerful, once the individual understands the connection between their problem and it's origin, the mind and soul starts to create a new energy flow to release the problem in this current lifetime. As you can see, love is so powerful, that even from one lifetime to another, it becomes a need that needs to be resolved and completed.

Sometimes, this lack of love or the experience of being hurt due to love can also manifest itself as a physical ailment or learning disability. A woman in her early fifties came to me for a reading late one afternoon. She was suffering from a disease called fibromyalgia, which can be extremely painful due to sensitivity to the nerves and muscles. It makes the body overly sensitive where a simple touch from someone else could cause incredible pain throughout the body.

As she spoke of her pain I could almost feel the daily struggles she had to endure just to handle simple everyday chores. As we started the reading, we quickly touched on the reason why this disease had connected with her. It seemed that five years earlier she went through a very difficult divorce. This divorce crushed her heart and soul so severely that she told herself she never wanted to feel again that strongly for another person. She never wanted to experience the pain again that she went through during her separation and eventual divorce. She never wanted to go through the humiliation of rejection, and she didn't want to hurt emotionally anymore. Her body listened to her demands, created a physical problem where these issues of not wanting to feel anymore inside was compensated by feeling too much outside, as in her physical body. Her emotional body didn't want to deal with the pain so it transferred it down to the physical body to deal with. So once again our angels try to show us that we truly are in charge of our lives, and that we manifest according to our needs, thoughts, fears, and desires. So to a certain degree, the statement which says, "Be careful what you wish for", can be applied to the two examples discussed above. We are co-creators in this world, and love plays such a crucial element in what we bring into our existence, either due to the lack, want, or expression of it.

Finally, we enter the discussion about spiritual love, the third level and most powerful. This is love for all that is beyond the physical plane. This is love for our angels, our God Source, our spiritual selves. This is truly the highest level of love, for in loving our spiritual being and all that connects us with spirit, we discover unconditional love. Countless experiences have been shared by individuals who have had a near death experience, and return to share with others how the level of love in the Spirit realm is beyond our comprehension. It is as though all our positive emotions and expressions of love are magnified a thousand times. I have spoken to many of these people who came close to death, and witnessed an entry into a beautiful place where total bliss and a sense of belonging were so strong. Some have encountered an experience with an angelic or spiritual being during this process ,and also express a sense of feeling a level of love unseen or felt in a human form. I myself, while battling a serious health issue ,found myself entering the Spirit state in my late twenties. I can say that the experience will never be forgotten. Imagine every possible positive emotion you can have and have it multiplied a thousand times. This is why so many people who encounter this experience, usually are disappointed when they realize they have to return to the physical world. Our Guardian angels hold a similar energy around them, because of the dimension in which they exist. In fact, many of my clients who come for an angel reading, tell me they feel a vibration or energy around them, the moment their angel enters and starts speaking to them. Obviously, it is not as strong as if they had entered the Spirit state, but still strong enough for them to feel a change or shift in the room.

    I once did a television show in Venezuela, where several famous Spanish actors and actresses were brought on stage so I could connect with their Guardian angel. I would take about five minutes with each one of them, describe their angel, and pass down a few messages for them. I had never met these people before, not even the day of the show, up until the moment they came on stage. This show was filmed in front of a live audience, I was extremely nervous because the show was in Spanish, and at that time my ability to speak Spanish fluently was a struggle. To make matters worse it was a popular show which aired to millions of viewers early in the morning. Throughout the show, every single person which I presented their angel to, ended up in tears. All of them said they felt this electrical charge of unconditional love surrounding them from their angel.

By the time the show was over, the camera men, the hostess, the audience, and some of the people working the control booth upstairs were also in tears. When the show aired, within three hours, I had received close to two hundred phone calls, e-mails, and faxes from people saying they had just watched the show, and were also in tears in their homes. Many called simply to thank me for allowing them to know that everyone had a guardian angel and they were not alone in this world. Others called to say they had a feeling that angels existed, but I was able to give them some proof to make that feeling more solid. This was an experience for me that I will hold inside forever, for it also fortified the need for humanity to know that there is unconditional love being given to us from Spirit, and from our angels. If we allow ourselves to accept it, it will assist us in enduring the difficult challenges in our lives, and create a sense of balance in our hearts. We need to learn not to blame ourselves for our decisions and mistakes in life, but realize just as our Guardian angels realize, that we are all doing the best we can and that in itself is more than OK.

Spiritual love is also that love that allows us to admire the beauty on our planet, and the miracles which are presented to us from time to time. It also allows us to respect other life forms and see that we all share a common thread in the creation of life. Spiritual love also allows us to accept life for what it brings, with no judgement, and with a sense of innocence.

Our angels also want us to understand that we come into this world by ourselves and eventually leave by ourselves. We have helpers as we come in, during our lives, and those waiting for us when we die. During the actual lifetime, when we are lucky enough to connect with love, those are the bonuses given to us, to allow us to discover ourselves and move forward. So if you had an incredible love partner for five years, twenty, or a lifetime, always cherish those memories, but be open to a new love connection. Never feel responsible for someone else's lack of love, or feel the need to stay in a loveless relationship, simply because they say they cannot live without you, when you do not share that same feeling. This is not a bulletin from the angels saying everyone should start divorcing. What I am saying, is that love is truly one of the greatest experiences you can have, and you should never lose out on the opportunity to discover it. Many couples, after a period of time, have outgrown the love for each other. Sometimes, it is their destiny to move forward, because in their karma, they have fulfilled whatever love responsibility this lifetime held for them. Staying in that loveless relationship only hurts the other person and yourself. First, everyone should make the effort to see if that spark still exists, and if it does, fight with every ounce of your being to ignite it again.

Love continues to be, and has always been the fuel for life regardless of the dimension or level of existence. If we, as human beings, can make love a priority to be felt and experienced whenever possible, we are ahead of the game. To extend one's love for another is to allow you to recognize how truly special we all are. The more we connect and discover self love, the more the chances of love becoming an everyday encounter in our lives, and the easier it becomes for us to understand and follow the paths which our angels have set in front of us. Regardless of what you have done in a negative way in the past or are doing presently, the love of our God Source will never punish or judge us, we are the ones too busy doing that to ourselves.

We are energies of love, trying to exist and make sense of our spiritual nature, upon a physical planet. The sooner we realize that love is what makes us different from material energy, the easier our transition to this higher vibration will be. Accept this new mergence with open arms, but more importantly with open hearts.

In the previous chapters containing messages from our Guardian angels, I have provided an exercise or activity to assist you in taking the message a little deeper into your hearts and mind. In this chapter I will do something different. I wish to simply share a poem I wrote in recognition of the love between us and our Guardian angels.

I SIMPLY AM....YOUR ANGEL

There is no need to always look back
for my task is to always be there for you
There truly is no need to ever feel lonely
You never walk alone, for I am part of you

On those days when you just can't bear anymore
I will choose to carry your burdens and worries
Those difficult days when you feel no one really cares
I will bring you back memories of being careless and free

When the pain gets unbearable, that tears just shed no more
I will lead you to laughter and even open the door
When your faith falters and your eyes simply cannot see
I will surround you with love and you will know it is me
For I am your angel of light, your angel of love
I am the hand that extends from high up above
I am the wings of your soul when you are ready to fly
I am the one you see right before death and again when you die

I simply am....your angel

Chapter 13

Time To React

As I mentioned in the beginning of this book, every one of the ten chapters carrying a message from our angels, has the potential of being a small book in itself. I have simply taken some of the highlights from many years of communicating with our Guardian angels and provided some thoughts, ideas, and tools that you can incorporate to assist you in this journey called life. As you reach this part of the book I hope that some of you have taken the time to review your own life, and see where you have an opportunity to make changes and seek new paths. Some of you will skip through and read only certain chapters which call your attention, others will read the book entirely, and feel a breath of fresh air, and still others will finish the book and feel nothing at all has changed in their life. Whatever you experience from this book is exactly what your angel wanted you to experience. Whatever direction the information provided has taken you to, is perfect for you. I did not choose to write this book to prove or validate the existence of Guardian angels, but rather, I wrote this book to validate the existence of yourself.

We are so lucky to be alive in a time when so much is taking place in our physical and spiritual existence. So much energy is being distributed in countless directions in this planet right now, and will continue to escalate regardless of your beliefs, fears, or doubts. We are going through a process in humanity where our spiritual bodies are finally awakening at a conscious level. If you were to truly understand what this represents it would actually touch your heart profoundly, and bring tears to your eyes. Tears of joy, of accomplishment, and tears of alliance with spirit would run through you as you realize the magnitude of what is taking place right now. For the first time in human existence, we are slowly being allowed to be our own guides, teachers, and spiritual foundations. It does not mean that we are being abandoned, just the opposite, we are graduating and taking on our own responsibility. Spirit is not leaving us to work things out on our own. It is joining forces with us to make the voyage easier and more effective. We have proven that mankind is capable and worthy of shedding our physical limitations and bringing about a new human consciousness unlike anything we have ever had in the past.

It is not coincidence that this book is being published and released at the end of the year 2006. The angels have told me that the year 2007 holds a great deal of changes. There are many individuals who decided to come into this world during these difficult times to assist humanity. These people consciously, in the spirit state, chose to be born in a human life and be in existence during these times. They wanted to be the ones responsible to help us gain the knowledge, the wisdom, the spirituality, the healing, and the courage, to turn things around and give our planet a second chance. These individuals are known as light workers. So many of these light workers are caring and loving people who just want to make a difference and help. Unfortunately, these people have had a very rough time over the last few years, in many areas, such as finances, love, health, relationships, work, and other areas. According to our angels, close to 50% or more of these light workers, around the world, will give up on their desire to assist humanity before the end of the year 2006. Those who hold onto their faith, overcome the many obstacles placed before them, and cross into 2007 with the same willingness to assist humanity, will start reaping their rewards. The years 2007 - 2012 is a period of changes in which many of these light workers will overcome blockages, have personal problems removed, and finally feel as though they are accomplishing their missions.

The year 2012 was always seen on the Mayan calender year, as the year in which the world was to shift. Many saw this as the end of civilization. In actuality, this is the beginning of a new development. It is a time when we can begin implementing new thoughts and ideas, such as the ones we talked about in the previous chapters, and start working towards group consciousness. There is an urgency in this matter, and we all need to participate in this development.

I would like to share an experience that happened to me around the age of twenty-one, and now, over twenty-seven years later, still continues to be processed mentally, emotionally, and energetically inside of me. I had been involved with the psychic group I mentioned before for almost a year, and the gentleman who led the group wanted to try an experiment with me. He was aware that I could tap into the spirit world, and he knew my body could hold a great deal of energy. He had been doing regressions, which is a hypnotic form of assisting individuals to remember their past lives, for many years. After close to a year of sharing and bonding with this group I had no problems with trying new adventures, especially in the psychic development area, and especially if it was a bit daring. He was fascinated with regression therapy and documented many of his cases. He wanted to see just how far back he could take an individual to conscious recollection of a past life. He had already done a regression on me that took me back to the 1500's in which I died in battle for religious crusades, so I was familiar with the process already. Not being a history buff, I had researched much of the information I disclosed in that regression, and was surprised to get much documented proof. We talked about the experiment and decided to get together in a small group the following Friday evening. I had total trust in this individual and seven of us got together promptly at seven in the evening that Friday.

Before we got started, we decided to connect a microphone to my shirt so whatever information which would come about could be recorded. Just as the first time, I was placed in a relaxed position, and in a state of deep mental relaxation. I was told to connect with my subconscious mind and retrieve a memory as far back as my soul had ever originated. Having worked with the power of the mind as a child, I quickly entered a state of hypnotic relaxation and just let myself go completely. Little did I know that this voyage would change my entire life. I could feel myself flowing backwards through time as though I was in a tunnel with no beginning or end. All I could see was glimpses of events, faces, and lights. This seemed to last for a few moments when suddenly I found myself in a level of energy unlike anything I had ever experienced.

As unbelievable as it may sound, I was transported back to a time when humanity, as a physical entity, had yet to be created. I had traveled back to reconnect with the God Source! All I could feel was the purest level of energy, love, and knowledge all wrapped together in pure perfection. To me it was like entering the heart of God. I had gone back to the beginning of time, before time even existed. I was aware of all thought, all feelings, and all that was, could be, and would be, all at the same time. It was the most awesome sensation of oneness anyone can possibly imagine. During this regression I began to explain in detail how the Source contained everything possible and the only thing it lacked was experience. As I discussed in Chapter nine, under the subject of mergence and the example of the ball of yarn, everything was a tight ball of perfection, but it had no sense of origin.

This God Source was all knowing but yet had no knowledge of how it became all knowing. In order to discover this, it had to unwind and digress itself energetically. It had to digress to it's simplest form possible in order to truly understand it's magnificence. Once it reached the simplest level it would hold on to it's memory, and start bringing it all back to the conscious level. For almost two hours I spoke, and explained the various levels and dimensions that needed to be created in order to accomplish this feat. As each level was recalled, it would gather all the experience it contained, and bring that to the next upcoming level. I had decided to follow this process all the way down to the human level, and be an active instrument to assist the God Source. Even as I spoke of all this information, in the back of my mind, I could not believe what I was saying and experiencing.

Finally, the gentleman performing the regression felt I had been under hypnosis long enough, it was time to end the process. It was important to now bring me back to my conscious level, especially due to the enormous amount of energy I was describing around me. Due to that energy, I had a difficult time coming out of the hypnosis. About fifteen minutes passed before I felt I was coming back into my physical body, and hearing his words to breath in deeply and open my eyes. Ten minutes later I was able to physically open my eyes, but yet could not see. All I could see was light vibrations, a few minutes later shapes and forms, but no details. Almost a half hour later, I finally was able to speak again and felt my senses connecting back. Everyone in the room was in a dead silence, as I finally started seeing their bodies and making out their faces. They had been in fear that something had happened to me, due to my delay in regaining consciousness. They were also astounded by the information I had provided.

We removed the microphone from my shirt and began to rewind the tape to make sure all the information had recorded. In the few paragraphs above, I only shared a very small percentage of what I actually shared with the group, while being recorded that evening. The cassette tape was stuck and the tiny mechanical instruments connected to the cassette recorder, which actually records the tape, was very hot. After further review, we realized some of the cassette recorder pieces surrounding the actual cassette looked as though it had melted. We were able to retrieve most of the tape, but apparently the energy of the place I had regressed to was so enormous, that it created an electrical short circuit, from my body, to the microphone, and to the cassette recorder. This energy was the one responsible for destroying part of the tape, and the recorder was useless after that.

That evening, after that regression, I was changed for the rest of my life. All the knowledge of all the levels or dimensions I had talked about, continued to trickle down into my conscious mind. Up to today, this continues to happen. What I really want to get across here is that your God, your Source, your belief of a supreme being, whatever it may be to you, is the highest level of love that can possibly be imagined. The level of love that I felt in that experiment, has never been reproduced in all my psychic and spiritual experiences since that day. The level of love we get from our Guardian angels is amazing, but yet it pales in comparison with the level of love from our God Source. These angels are an extension of this Source and so are we! Every one of us is a particle, an element, a powerful connection of all that is and will be. When you truly understand what I am saying here, then you can truly understand the value of your own individual existence.

Our Guardian's main message to humanity is that we are part of the purity of God. They want us to realize how important our lives are, and especially, how important the experiences we encounter on a daily basis are. We are the first level of conscious thinking life forms to start working our way back to the Source. As we merge with the Spirit realm and release our physical limitations, we will have started the cycle to become one, once again. This is why so many other dimensional levels are paying so much attention to what is happening in our planet. We are the brave ones that have finally evolving to a higher level of consciousness. We are finally realizing that we do not have to return to another physical life once we feel our soul has attained all possible human experiences. Once we gain this mergence, as an entire planet, then the next level will follow, and so on and so on, until all conscious forms of life have reunited with the beauty and love of God.

Understanding and appreciating your own life has always been the number one purpose or role which our Guardian angels try to teach us. From the beginning of humanity, these heavenly beings have been trying to assist us in loving ourselves so much that we no longer needed to suffer. We can, as a group, gather all our experiences, take it to the spirit level, and begin this incredible evolution. But it takes every one of us, as a unit, or the transition cannot take place. To be complete, every soul has to evolve, therefore you are an intricate part of this plan. We still have a great deal of work ahead of us, and many of us will not see the major changes in our lifetimes. We do need to start planting the seeds for those that will follow us. All of us are responsible for carrying our own load whether it is this lifetime or the next ten. As we carry our own load, we will start lifting the burdens of others and assist each other in a common goal.

Whichever words in this book resonate with your heart and soul, allow them to be the first conscious words to alert you in becoming sensitive to a process that is already taking place within humanity. Allow the unconditional love from your Guardian to be an extension of the unconditional love you can give to your fellow man. Allow yourself to be part of that ripple effect, which will eventually join all our hearts in a flow of majesty and love, that so many forms of life, in so many dimensions anxiously await. Everyone living today, regardless of your occupation, belief, or level in society, is subconsciously joined together in this beautiful plan. By discovering ways to bring this love and information to your daily conscious level, you, in your own way, can speed the process for all of us.

Our Guardian angels wish for us to take the initiative to create changes for ourselves and others in a positive way. Begin to take on the responsibility you have been given as co-creators on this planet, and merge together in order for love to be the conqueror of fear. Realize that this process cannot be done without the assistance of everyone. Since all of us are an extension of the God Source, all of us carry an essential element, an element essential in completing the cycle. As our energies begin to escalate, make an attempt to tap into your own abilities, therefore assisting others around you as well. Let us make our lives the best possible by respecting the energies of all life forms, and respecting the similarities and differences we all have. We also need to respect the physical planet, and nurture it for it has been nurturing us since the beginning.

Realize no matter how difficult your journey may be, you never travel it alone, not now or ever. Learn to communicate and speak with your Guardian angels as you would to your most trusted friend. Break through all barriers of communication so you can begin to feel the love and comfort your angel is constantly pouring into your existence. Remember, it starts with self love, self discovery, and the desire to truly be the spiritual being you have always been. Look around and take the time to view and review your life, your accomplishments, your fears, and your goals. Give yourself permission to start removing some of those fears and try new adventures. Become sensitive to your life purpose, trust your heart and instinct, and follow your dreams. None of your time has ever been wasted. The time ahead of you can now be more direct, fulfilling, and meaningful. May the love poured in this book provide you with an opening paragraph to your own book of life. Start your journey alongside your Guardian angel and really feel and experience all you can in life. I wish you all a wondrous journey totally surrounded with love and empty of fear.

    I mentioned in the beginning of this book that other areas of messages had been provided to me from our Guardian angels, which I plan to share at a later date. Many of these messages deal with future events and changes in such areas as religion, government, education, family structure, new dimensions, technology, communication, and many others. I will share information about old helpers who have been assisting us for some time, such as extraterrestrials. In my own journey, I have had the pleasure of meeting other teachers and students who have confirmed many of the messages shared here, and which have also confirmed that we never stop learning. I still need to continue my work, not only with Guardian angels, but with humanity in general. May we spread our wings, and touch each other in flight, as we fly together to our home that awaits us with love.

About the Author

The author eventually left his position, after nearly twenty years as a business executive, to pursue his lifetime passion to teach, heal, and work with humanity in the understanding of Spiritual truth. Martin Crespo was gifted as a child with psychic and healing abilities. He overcame his fear of seeing spirits and angels, and with the gift of healing at the age of twelve, he quickly learned his life would not take a normal path.

Today, Martin has combined his talents, and has become an adjunct professor of Metaphysics and Spiritual healing at the college level. He has appeared on numerous Spanish Television programs demonstrating his ability to connect with Guardian Angels. His work has also been featured on many magazines, such as Cosmopolitan, Ocean Drive, as well as newspapers. Thousands have seen him for private consultations where he assists many in discovering their life path and initiates the release of physical, emotional, and spiritual blockages. Today Martin Crespo provides lectures and workshops as he continues to handle personal clients from around the world. He resides in Miami, Florida with his wife and son.

Made in the USA
Columbia, SC
25 February 2019